Building Refurbishment
- How Commercial Building Owners Increase Their Real Estate Value

Special Case Studies of Singapore Marina Bay Area and Orchard Road

JOSH NG

PARTRIDGE
A Penguin Random House Company

To order additional copies of this book, contact
Toll Free 800 101 2657 (Singapore)
Toll Free 1 800 81 7340 (Malaysia)
orders.singapore@partridgepublishing.com

www.partridgepublishing.com/singapore

DEDICATED TO

My family especially my wife
who is with me throughout this life journey.

ACKNOWLEDGEMENT

Peck Hong for her encouragement
Jesselyn, Simon, Mr Chia who helped reviewed the book
My students whom I have also learnt much from
Ngee Ann Polytechnic who provided an opportunity for me to explore
this subject further

C O N T E N T S

INTRODUCTION

Building Refurbishment is getting more common nowadays. This is especially so in the developed countries whereby a faster turnaround time is required for constructing a new building. Thus it makes commercial sense to adapt an existing building instead of developing it from ground up. In other situations the local regulations may not allow a building to be demolished due to conservation efforts or advocacy. Building Refurbishment may also be necessary to renew and update a building in response to meeting "green" standards or universal design requirements, for example, incorporating handicap access. It is also an exercise often practised by real estate fund manager to enhance their building value.

How do building owners increase their real estate value? Building Refurbishment is one major way to do that. Particularly for commercial buildings which derive their real estate value by earning recurring rental income. Hence if one can physically change the design and capacity of the building to increase its rental income, wouldn't the building's real estate value increase? Most probably, however with risks involved.

This book covers the essential concepts of Building Refurbishment and its strategies to increase real estate value. It differs from most technical books on building adaptation which focus on the technology involved or architectural books which focus on the design aspect. This book is written to uncover the relationship between a seemingly technical project and the building performance and value within the context of real estate. Major case studies and lessons will be drawn from

Singapore using it as an example of what most developed cities are probably facing also in terms of Building Refurbishment.

Other important lessons and concepts on how to measure Building Refurbishment, manage Building Refurbishment and the regulatory impact will also be examined.

CHAPTER 1

What Drives Building Refurbishment?

Learning Objective

- To appreciate the different perspectives surrounding the forces driving Building Refurbishment
- To better understand the changes in environment and how buildings respond to these changes

1.0   Context of this book

This book is written for all who are interested to understand how building's real estate value increases through Building Refurbishment. It focuses particularly on commercial buildings which I loosely defined as any buildings which fetch rental income. The main coverage of this book is in the area of commercial Building Refurbishment. We will look at its context, motivation, strategies, measures of success, risk management and regulatory impact.

A building is after all unlike an interior space or an apartment. Apartment owners for example could (almost) do anything he or she likes in renovating the apartment. A building is however often heavily regulated by local authorities. Similarly any construction activities are also very heavily regulated. This is where value can be created. The context of this book is based on the premise that commercial building value is enhanced by managing the difficult process of refurbishment. And while not everyone is a building owner, one can still draw lessons from this book if he or she

- intends to buy a building
- is not from the real estate industry and would like to know how real estate value is enhanced through asset enhancement i.e. Building Refurbishment
- works for real estate companies or building owners
- is an architect or designer
- is a real estate marketing person marketing the sale of a building
- owns not a building but an apartment or smaller space and wants to see how you can apply some of the lessons here to your situation

Most of the concepts and lessons here are drawn from my own professional experiences and observations as well as news articles and reports. As such, the geographical context of this book is Singapore. However this is probably similar to many developed cities experiencing the need to renew their cities.

1.1. The changing world we live today

A good way to analyse the potential environmental impact on the building and its performance is to use the PEST analysis. PEST stands for:-

P – Political
E – Economic
S – Social
T - Technology

If we look at the last 30 or 20 years or even 10 years, the world we live in is changing and changing at a faster speed. One of the concepts of real estate is that it is a product driven by "derived demand". What this means is that if there is a demand for a certain physical environment, we then build that physical environment. And with the use of that environment, the value of it is hence derived. For example, all of us need to shop or to buy our groceries, watch movies etc. Therefore a shopping mall is built to meet that demand. Hence when the economic or social environment changes over time, our demand for the same shopping mall we used to shop in the last 10 to 20 years may change.

Any change in the operating environment of commercial properties may impact its earning potential. This in turn impacts its annual net operating income and hence its capital value based on the capitalization rule.

This change in demand can be due to the rise in the number of the middle income earners. More people may now have more disposable income and eat out more often. Therefore there is now a greater demand for restaurants and cafes which require different building services e.g. food smell or cooking exhaust. This then triggers the building owner to decide to either refurbish the building or to tear the building down and rebuild.

Drawing on the same principle stated above, any change in the operating environment of commercial properties may impact its earning potential. This in turn impacts its annual net operating income and hence its capital value based on the capitalization rule :-

Commercial building capital value = Net operating income / investor's yield

Some of recent social, economic and demographic trends impacting the potential earning capacity of the commercial properties are as follows:-

Building Type	Environmental changes
Office buildings	• Re-structuring of economy into more service oriented industry – leading to an increase demand for high specifications and technology office building for the financial sector. • The exponential thirst for ever more energy to house data • The use of thermal resistant façade to lower energy bill in cooling the building
Shopping Malls	• The decline of certain trade or reduced demand for certain products leading to the re-configuration of shopping malls. Eg the expansion of Apple stores and decline of DVD, CD shops. • 2008 financial crisis – leading to the exit of Carrefour from some countries and the aggressive regional expansion of other retailers into Asia e.g. Uniqolo, H&M • Consolidation of large format department store and the proliferation of different store format
Industrial buildings	• Re-configuration to cater to changing industry specifications e.g. addition of ramp for trucks to reach the upper floors directly to the units' doorstep, loading / unloading bay or higher floor loading
Hotels	• Upgrading of guestroom design to incorporate latest entertainment and business technology eg wall mounted Smart TV, wireless internet • Upgrading of finishes and fittings to keep up with competition arising from increase tourist arrivals and higher expectations. There is now even a 7 star hotel!

Any progressive major building owners would need to understand their current positioning of their real estate portfolio. They would also monitor the market trends (PEST) to gauge its potential economic impact. Should the economic performance of the commercial properties fall below expectation, then it is time to consider Building Refurbishment as one of the possible options to enhance performance.

1.2 The world changes. People change. Buildings also change

What drives Building Refurbishment? We can argue that it is the people who drive it. The people designing the building also make changes in the way buildings are designed and constructed over time. In the older days more than 50 years ago it was very common to have masonry buildings. And it was only about 50-70 years ago we started to have a lot of reinforced concrete buildings. Only about 20-50 years ago we started to have a lot more structural steel buildings cladded with glass façade.

With better design and technology there are now more high-rise buildings. Hence building owners of buildings more than 10-20 years old or low rise building may want to:-

- Increase the building capacity by adding more floors
- Refresh and renew their buildings to have a more updated look and feel and greater performance and functions

People change. Buildings can also change because of our change in perception of the way we use the buildings. We now realise that we need to be a responsible and inclusive global citizens because of the climate change and diverse population. Hence our buildings would also change to meet such aspirations. Therefore building owners respond by "greening" the building and constructing handicap friendly features in the building. A very common and valuable option is to re-façade the building.

It not only gives a more modern look to the building, it also reduces its energy bill with less heat entering the building (in the case of tropical countries). This indirectly improves the real estate value.

1.3   Chasing the dollars

The ultimate objective of any building owner is either to retain or increase his building real estate value. Any progressive real estate companies would consider the life cycle of their buildings in terms of their real estate value :-

- Has the existing building reached its fullest potential? Can the building performance be enhanced e.g. by further borrowing or more aggressive marketing strategies or physical changes to the building design
- Does the acquisition target have any potential that is not realized by existing owners and so upon buying over the new owner could refurbish and reap this potential value?

In both ways, if in the opinion of the building owner the building is not performing, often Building Refurbishment is an option to consider.

This is especially so for most Real Estate Investment Trust ("REIT") management companies. They manage the real estate portfolio for REITs shareholders and are responsible for monitoring the building performance. Private real estate fund managers also fall into this category.

Most of the times the management fee of these fund managers are closely tied to the performance of the commercial buildings. Moreover some of the fund managers may also earn additional fee for project management during the commercial Building Refurbishment.

1.4   Time is money

Time is money. That is only if time has become more valuable than money itself. This is the case when the opportunity cost in terms of time lost is higher than the cost of refurbishing a building. The situation is even more acute when the building being refurbished is a very high yield building or has a very short lease left. Let's take an example from Singapore:-

- An old dilapidated horse racing complex is left vacant as the government decided to relocate it to the outskirt as it is sitting within a prime land and causing traffic jam to its vicinity.
- The horse racing complex is located within a high end residential district and the government decided to lease it out to a master tenant for retail use and enrichment centers for the residents nearby. It has an allowable net usable retail space of 350,000 square feet besides a huge 3,000 lot car-park and a car mall selling second hand car occupying another net usable space of 400,000 square feet.
- The master tenant has a short lease of only three years with an option to renew for another two more terms of three years each. A total of nine years.
- The latest master tenant paid $1,065,678 per month for their first term and has sunk in about $18 million in refurbishment cost. This works out to about $18.8 million every year assuming the $18 million refurbishment cost is amortized over 3 years of the first tenancy term.
- A $1.30 psf is charged for the car mall or a total of $6.24 million turnover per year.
- According to my calculation the retail space charges about $6.65 per square feet and with 80% occupancy, the turnover for the retail portion is about $22.34 million per year. Combined with the car mall, its annual turnover is $28.58 million. Car-parking is free.

In the above situation the refurbished horse racing complex (which is no longer used for horse racing) earns the master tenant an estimated gross high yield of 52% per year ($28.58 million over $18.8 million). Given a short tenure of 9 years there is no point to redevelop. In this case, the building owner or rather master tenant is earning an estimated 1.52 times of every dollar he puts monthly. This is necessary in order to recover the cost of refurbishment. It is therefore necessary to complete the refurbishment as soon as possible and is estimated to recover its refurbishment cost of $18 million by year 1 excluding the master tenancy rental of about $1 million per month. Way before the lease term is up for renewal by the end year 3.

1.5   Competition

Competition is a major driving force which pushes building owners towards refurbishment. This is in order to renew or re-position their buildings. The push is especially strong when the competition for users or tenants is most intense. This can happen when

- The building is a shopping mall
- The building is located within an area with other similar buildings eg the central business district or financial centre or a major shopping belt or tourist belt

In Chapter 5 later I will attempt to explain how competition drives various major building owners to refurbish within the Marina Bay area as well as Orchard Road in Singapore.

Under such circumstances... refurbishment is no longer a case of building obsolescence or the desire to 'green' the building. It is a case of retaining tenants and maintaining or improving the building rental income.

Under such circumstances mentioned above, refurbishment is no longer a case of building obsolescence or the desire to 'green' the building. It is a case of retaining tenants and maintaining or improving the building rental income. Some of which can be driven by REITs fund manager. Even though the refurbishment needs to be completed speedily, the primary motivation is differentiation and survival.

A case in point is Singapore Suntec City / Convention Centre which spent a massive SGD410 million on refurbishment from 2012 and to be completed in 2015. SGD410 million is enough to build about 150 high end apartments or buy almost 2.5 hectare of land for residential development in suburbs of Singapore. I believe the large amount of refurbishment cost spent is in respond to the opening of Marina Bay Sands in 2009 - a 5 million squre feet development including the best in class convention centre - and the impending opening of South Beach City between 2015 to 2016 just next to Suntec City - a 1.58 million sqft mixed development led by City Development Limited. Both are big enough to compete against the older Suntec City/ Convention Centre.

Another interesting observation under those two circumstances I mentioned in this section is that competition forces building owners to refurbish MORE frequently. In a typical scenario whereby the world did not change much or the user requirements or taste or purchasing power did not change much, a building would only experience refurbishment upon reaching building obsolescence or redundancy. Such obsolescence or redundancy typically happens for a building after many years. In terms of physical obsolescence it could be 50-70 years. Economic obsolescence could take about 20 years. That is not the case for an under-performing building facing intense competition. This is especially if such building is owned by progressive real estate companies or REITs who are more financially driven. Suntec City opened in 1997 and had its major refurbishment in 2012 about

15 years since its opening. In fact there were several smaller refurbishments even before 2012.

1.6   Obsolescence and redundancy

We have examined several factors driving buildings for refurbishment. They are

- Environmental changes
- Buildings responding to change in building design and requirements
- Motivation from financial returns
- Motivation from early completion of development instead of re-development
- Competition

I would say that the first two factors – environmental changes and building responding to new requirements and design – are more of the "traditional" drivers of building refurbishment. These tend to be related to building obsolescence and redundancy.

Obsolescence of a building is a decline in the usefulness of the building. Redundancy of a building occurs when there is decrease in demand for a particular type of property leading to excess capacity e.g. the use of auditorium within an office building. It can be rather confusing to understand the difference between the concept of building obsolescence and redundancy. Both relate to the decline of the use of a building. Whilst "obsolescence" is a macro phenomenon, "redundancy" reflects the reduce use of a certain type of real estate space.

The decline in the building usage is often reflected in its rentability and rental value. As a certain type of real estate space become redundant, its rental value also decline and becomes less competitive or unattractive for prospective tenants. For example the redevelopment of several standalone cinemas built in the past. Cinemas these days are housed within a shopping mall.

As the building age, while the physical structure itself is still standing, several of the building elements have deteriorated e.g. building services – lifts and air conditioning, architectural products – doors and finishes etc. Hence instead of piecemeal or cyclical maintenance for the building, a total overhaul in the form of Building Refurbishment may be required to arrest the building decline.

1.7   When building refurbishment is the ONLY option

Building refurbishment is the ONLY option available to a building owner when the building is a conserved building. Assuming the intention of the owner is to either increase the building performance or value. Such building cannot be demolished completely and local regulation requires the building owner to protect and even enhance certain building elements.

A very common situation is the preservation of historical building facade. Special refurbishment technology is required to retain such facade. Special trademen may also need to be sourced to restore the former glory of the facade. Since such building is built typically more than 50 years ago the building owner may need to strengthen the structural integrity of the building as it could be near physical obsolescence. This is especially so when additional floor is added thereby increasing the building load.

1.8   Whose perspective?

So what drives Building Refurbishment? It depends whose perspective we are looking from. It is also defined by other project related factors e.g. time, cost and quality.

Type of building owners	Driver for Building Refurbishment
Progressive real estate companies	Financial yield

REITs fund managers (representing the REITs shareholders) and private real estate fund manager	Yield and fee driven
Owners or master tenants of short lease building	Payback and time
Owners of shopping mall or within a major shopping, tourist or financial belt	Competition
Owners of physically or economically obsolete buildings	Maintenance, change of use or re-positioning for higher yield
State owned conserved buildings	Maintenance, urban renewal
Private owners of conserved buildings	Differentiation in real estate product offering, change of use for higher yield

1.9   Summary

In summary we examine the context surrounding Building Refurbishment and attempted to understand the driving forces behind such refurbishment. Essentially it depends on whose perspective and what type of building owners as well the type of building owned. Generally most building owners are affected by environmental changes which then warrant Building Refurbishment as the building age. While that is true, there are other forces which drive Building Refurbishment, particularly competition surrounding commercial buildings.

CHAPTER 2

Measuring Building Refurbishment

Learning Objective

- To learn how to measure Building Refurbishment objectively.
- To understand how to carry out feasibility studies of Building Refurbishment.

2.1 Appreciate the varying scope, scale and definition of building refurbishment

Refurbishment is any work done on an existing building in order to extend its useful life through adaptation to provide a new and updated version of the original structure. It could also involve building performance enhancement e.g. its air conditioning system as part of the owner's thrive for greener building. There are numerous types of Building Refurbishment. Some of the common terminologies are:-

- Conversion
- Conservation
- Restoration
- Retrofitting
- Renovation
- Addition & Alteration (A&A)

We may be confused by these different terminologies. Strictly speaking they are all different. However, as there are no precise definitions to differentiate these terminologies, they tend to be used loosely. For clearer differentiation purpose, we can for instance categorize them by:-

- owner's motivation (see Chapter 1)
- commercial or non-commercial
- the different level of conservation
- the scale and time taken for the work
- the extent of intervention in the existing building fabric
- the extent of structural change and demolition
- user / occupier management

There are some differences between commercial properties and non-commercial properties refurbishment. Commercial properties refurbishment generally refers to those buildings which are used for generating rental income or business e.g. malls, offices, hotels, industrial buildings etc. As for non-commercial properties they could be residential buildings or institutional buildings e.g. museums, schools, churches etc.

There is also a specific category of buildings – conservation or preserved buildings which may either fall under commercial use or non-commercial use. An example of conserved building converted to commercial use is The Fullerton Hotel in Singapore which was previously the General Post Office. It was built in the 1920s. The up and coming National Art Gallery in Singapore is a combination of two preserved buildings – former Supreme Court and the Parliament House.

Such conserved or preserved buildings refurbishment tend to make use of more advanced refurbishment technologies – under-pinning, re-façade, over-roofing etc. in addition to the possible building extensions. A specialized area of building refurbishment is the restoration of shophouses which involves termite treatment, strengthening and fire-proofing of timber floor hoist and specialized tradesman for façade art work.

While there is no universal definition for the various types of Building Refurbishment, it helps to us to grasp its implications better if we understand the scale and extend, its project duration and cost. A small residential house refurbishment would probably have less complication as compared to a major shopping mall refurbishment. This is also not comparable to a major refurbishment of a preserved monument being converted to a hotel.

2.2   David Kincaid Concept

What I find by far the easiest way to measure Building Refurbishment is to consider the concept presented by David Kincaid. In his book *"Adapting Buildings For Changing Uses"* *(2002)*, he illustrated a simple two dimensions matrix to measure Building Refurbishment:-

- the intervention to the building fabric which is its facade and
- the modification to the building structure.

Any major Building Refurbishment which involves the change of façade or structural horizontal or vertical extension is considered "high" change and is therefore a very major Building Refurbishment. From such measurement we could derive four basic strategies for physically changing the building:-

	Maintain External Fabric	Replace External Fabric
MODIFICATION:- Internal Space Only	Low change	Low-medium Change
RECONFIGURATION:- Space & Structure	Medium-high Change	High Change

Figure 2.1 – David Kincaid (2002) concept

I have re-interpreted David Kincaid's matrix as follows:-

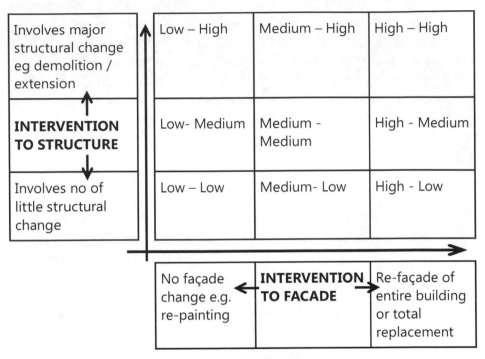

Involves major structural change eg demolition / extension	Low – High	Medium – High	High – High
INTERVENTION TO STRUCTURE	Low- Medium	Medium - Medium	High - Medium
Involves no of little structural change	Low – Low	Medium- Low	High - Low

No façade change e.g. re-painting	**INTERVENTION TO FACADE**	Re-façade of entire building or total replacement

Figure 2.2 – Re-interpreted matrix David Kincaid (2002) concept

The re-interpreted of the David's Kincaid's concept gives some clarity on the extent of intervention to the structure and the building's façade which is its fabric.

A low façade intervention could be mere re-painting. A medium façade intervention could be partial re-façade and a high intervention is a total replacement of the building's entire façade.

A low structure intervention could be mere wall or floor penetration for the purpose of installing M&E services and the existing structural design and pattern is not disturbed. A high structure intervention could involve more than 50% change to the building's structure eg floor and relocation of columns etc.

The more extensive is the change of use, the more intensive is the intervention to the building structure and design. As a result, the more extensive is the demolition work. Consequently the greater is the cost and inconvenience caused and the project duration is expected to be longer.

The more extensive is the change of use, the more intensive is the intervention to the building structure and design.

Replacing the external fabric is the same as re-cladding. It could also involve over-cladding which is new façade work without removing existing façade. Rather the new façade is cladded over the existing ones. This is similar to roofing works. Most of us are already familiar with re-roofing works – a replacement of the waterproofing or heat insulation layer of a roof. Sometimes in the context of Building Refurbishment, a building may have "over-roofing". This can be the case in two situations:-

- a new and different roofing system completely covers over a failing flat roof and acts as the primary roof protection.
- a long-span glazing system which stretches over an entire building atrium to shelter the atrium or cover it entirely to produce usable space.

A modification of internal space without any façade change would be similar to a major renovation or fit-out for a major commercial office unit

The modified matrix in Figure 2.2 provides a framework to measure the extent of changes to a building. More examples will be provided in Chapter 3.

David Kincaid (2002) further relates his matrix to six development options. These are the options available for a building owner facing declining building performance:-

1. make the building more flexible as it is (without much refurbishment)
2. make the building more flexible with some adaptation
3. adapt the entire building in its vacant state without demolition
4. adapt the building with some demolition to suit new use
5. adapt the building with some structural extensions horizontally or vertically
6. demolish and rebuild the building to suit entirely the new use

Low change strategy falls within option 1 and 2 and high change strategy falls within option 4, 5 and 6.

2.3   Extension

It would be necessary at this point to explain what is meant by "extension" in Building Refurbishment. "Extension" is a rather strange English word to be used to describe Building Refurbishment.

Extension of a building in the literal sense really means extending the building in terms of expanding its physical form. This physical extension can be done either horizontally or vertically.

It may seem like a simple exercise to extend the building. One would possibly think of it like a lego block just stacking one on top of another. IT IS NOT THAT SIMPLE. Several considerations are required. See below:-

Considerations when carrying "extensions"	Implications
Legislation related to planning control	• Increase in gross floor area which may attract development charge by the government.
Building code related	• It is almost like a construction project and there is a possibility that the building may be under the old building code which causes some incompatibility.
Tenancy related	• Possible incompatible tenancy mix • Project management issue as existing tenants may still be in the building.

Technical Considerations

Perhaps the two greatest concerns a building owner may have when embarking on a building extension are:-

- design considerations
- the integration of the "old" and "new" part of the building.

Some of the design considerations would be:-

- Positioning of new space
- New Internal layout
- Daylight penetration
- Aesthetics for the enlarged building layout and façade design
- Massing – the bulking effect of the extension on neighboring properties
- Form of construction – compatibility with the original building
- Interface of the old and new
- Weather-tightness
- Impact on circulation

Integration of the "old" and "new" is of particular importance as any "new" extension is mostly not a standalone structure. As such in order to have a usable, functional and pleasant "extension", it must be connected and integrated with the existing building in various ways:-

- Building services connection and integration
- Leveling
- Use of finishes
- Character of the old and new
- Use of frame and structures
- Structural integrity

Of all the factors involved in the integration of the "old" and "new", structural integrity impacts life and safety. Hence structural integrity must be maintained at all times even during the construction period. Several structural considerations are required depending on the scope and location of building refurbishment.

If the building refurbishment is a horizontal extension and the new extension is more or less a standalone structure, then it must be able to take its own load with new foundation design. Perhaps there could be some lateral load transfer in the linkage between the old and new structure but such loading is secondary as compared to the new structure own structural and foundation design.

If the building refurbishment is a part of the existing building and not standalone, structural consideration must be made as to the load bearing capacity of the existing structure. If the existing structure cannot bear the addition load, transfer beam to other columns or additional piling or micro piling is required. The existing floor plate of the building could be enlarged.

Another possible scenario is vertical extension of the building. In such situation the existing column grid design is very crucial in determining whether such extension is practical. Usually the vertical extension relies on these existing columns for load transfer to the foundation. If these existing columns do not have the capacity then these columns needs to be enhanced structurally. See Figure 2.3 for an example of vertical upward extension of an office building in Singapore – 111 Somerset.

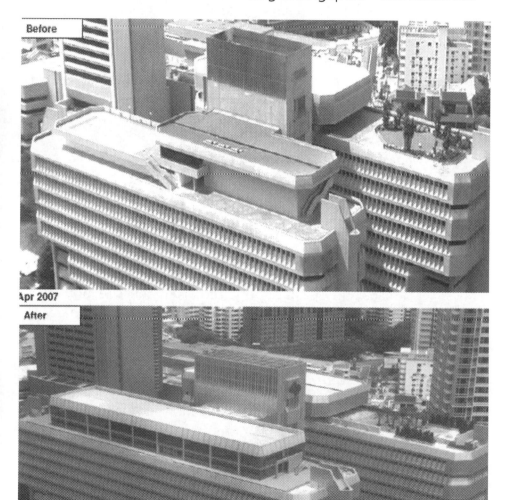

Figure 2.3 – Vertical extension of 111 Somerset previously called Singapore Power Building, 2007

2.4   Horizontal / Vertical / Combined Extension

In terms of horizontal extension there could be:-

- Front extension
- End extension
- Side extension

In terms of vertical extension there could be:-

- Upward extension on top of the building
- Downward extension with deeper basement construction underneath the building

Upward extension could arise from:-

- being part of the re-roofing or over-roofing project as in case of a residential loft construction.
- site constraints from the site boundary which limit the amount of site area available for horizontal extension. This is typical of high-rise buildings whereby there is usually a set-back required from the site boundary. There must also be sufficient space for building access and circulation. Hence there is little site area left for horizontal extension.

Downward basement extension is uncommon. This is because of the substantial cost involved in excavation, temporary structural support and waterproofing of existing and new structure. In addition during the excavation process, further care needs to be taken to handle the ingress of ground water and higher construction safety risk. There is also the risk of structural impact arising from soil differential settlement. However when there is height control over the building and there is limited site area for expansion, basement extension is the only logical option for increasing the building floor area. Other important consideration is the need to provide fire escape route, ventilation and also daylight where possible for basement.

An example of downward extension is I12 Katong in Singapore (Figure 2.4) whereby additional one storey of basement carpark is added to the building. In addition, its front façade was horizontally extended outwards at level 2. An additional one to two stories are also added at the back of the building to accommodate a cinema.

In most major Building Refurbishment however the extension involved is a combined extension. Both horizontal and vertical extensions are involved as in the case of I12 Katong mall in Figure 2.4. In the downtown area of developed cities, this may be increasingly common as cities' building owners build downwards to connect to the cities' underground train network.

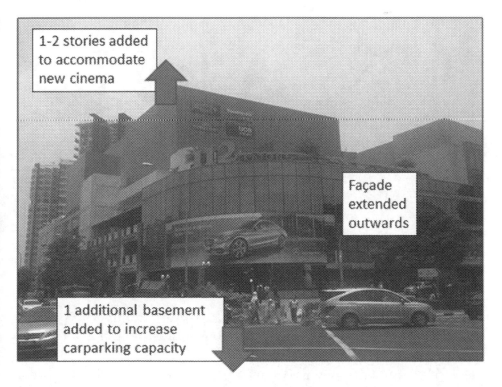

Figure 2.4 – Combined extensions of new I12 Katong in Singapore

2.5   Measuring Building Refurbishment Feasibility

Based on the David Kincaid (2002) concept and having understood how building extension is carried out, we could start to understand at least one aspect of Building Refurbishment feasibility study - practicality. This aspect examines the technical and construction aspect of a proposed Building Refurbishment.

Before any real estate companies or building owners embark on building refurbishment, a detailed feasibility studies is required to ensure the investment is well spent. Feasibility study is the study of the Building Refurbishment project to evaluate if the returns in terms of value or benefit created are worth the investment or cost spent based on investor's rate of return. Expected returns must be greater than the cost spent.

Primarily we consider three main types of feasibility when evaluating and planning for building refurbishment:-

- Practicality – technical, constructional aspect
- Utility – functional and design aspect
- Economic viability – discounted cash flow

Some of the practicality considerations are:-

- The existing use of the building
- Whether the building is a conservation building
- Accessibility to the site – tight site requires careful planning for delivery of equipment and materials. It may also increase the construction cost.

Utility is examining the functional and design aspect of a building. A refurbished building should meet the intended new or existing use of the building in terms of the spatial and environmental needs. For example the conversion of old schools into office requires additional electrical load. The conversion of an office building into a hotel may not be ideal as the ceiling height may be restricted by the old structural design.

Generally this involves having a sense of space and design, couple with an understanding of the various design typologies for various type of building use. For instance a hotel would require 15-25 square metre for each guestroom with a window bay. A shopping mall would usually require an atrium for events and activity generating. Does the existing structural grid allow modification to suit the new intended use?

Floor ceiling height will also have an impact on building refurbishment. If the existing floor ceiling height is low, it may not be ideal for conversion to most other use e.g. retail store, hotel guestroom, office unit as they usually have mechanical and electrical requirements which takes up ceiling space. The minimum habitable clearance height is 2.4m in Singapore.

Yet another consideration is the design of circulation whether for the users or for fire escape purpose. A restaurant for example needs to plan the circulation from the kitchen to the dining table to food disposal and for the customer to move from the waiting area to the dining table to the cashier. In the case of a large building refurbishment, the building owner would also need to consider the shoppers and car-park circulation and fire escape routes.

Economic viability

The building refurbishment project is only economically viable when the expected future property value is greater than the anticipated project cost.

Three common methods of measuring economic feasibility are:-

- Net Present Value
- Internal Rate of Return
- Payback period

In order to arrive at a decision to conduct Building Refurbishment, the number crunching for economic feasibility must be conducted as accurately as possible. This involves collecting several sources of information from:-

- the building management – existing floor area, tenancy, rental rate
- the marketing team – projected increase in rental rate
- the construction team – new floor design and area, construction cost
- other sources – e.g. the finance department to provide the cost of financing etc.

The various computations are best done using Microsoft Excel and involve calculating the project revenue and cost:-

Projected revenue

- the project rental / benefit arising from the increased area (if applicable) arising from the refurbishment
- the increased rental rate arising from the re-positioning of the new space after refurbishment
- possible vacancy rate/ take up rate

Projected cost

- the cost of development – construction, consultant free, authorities fee, development charge if any, site management cost for minimizing disturbance, temporary works cost etc
- marketing cost
- taxation e.g. income tax
- cost of financing if any
- projected operating cost after completion of refurbishment

All the figures should be expressed on an annual basis to deduce the net operating income of the building after refurbishment until the end of its lease period. These annual figures are then expressed in today's value using a discount rate. This discount rate could be the investor's expected rate of return or the capitalization yield or an assumed rate depending on how one evaluate the discounting process. Such tedious process is best carried out using an Microsoft Excel spreadsheet.

The Microsoft Excel spreadsheet developed would then be able to calculate the three measures of economic feasibility:-

- Net Present Value – the cumulative total of the difference between the revenue and cost
- Internal Rate of Return – the required rate of total return if the net present value is zero
- Payback period – the number of years of net operating income to recover the refurbishment project cost

Such Microsoft Excel spreadsheet is useful when we would like to test several scenario or variables. For e.g.:-

- the discount rate to adopt to discount all figures to the present value
- the number of economic life years for calculating the feasibility
- the change in rental rate if any to incorporate rental growth or decline
- or the various design scheme and their cost

Economic feasibility is the primary decision criteria for determining whether to proceed with the building refurbishment. Often the practicality and utility feasibility carried out would be translated into some form of cost to be incorporated into the economic feasibility. For instance, if there is site constraint then the cost of construction would increase. Or if the existing typology is not suitable for the new use then we may have to alter its structural design to fit the new design.

So how do we decide if the results we crunched are acceptable? Different building owners or investors may have different benchmark for the above three economic feasibility indicators – NPV, IRR and payback period. It may depends the owners'/ investors' existing cost of financing, non-tangible returns eg image and branding, whether if it is for owners' occupation etc.

There is however a risk that the intended building refurbishment may not translate into the envisaged increase in rental income. After all, the project rental income increase is based on best effort market studies which may be wrong.

One thing to note is that there is a difference between a typical economic feasibility and that for Building Refurbishment project. Building Refurbishment economic feasibility seeks to find out the difference in revenue and operating cost <u>BEFORE</u> and <u>AFTER</u> the refurbishment. In that way we could truly evaluate whether the refurbishment project is worth spending.

2.6   Summary

With the understanding of building extensions in Chapter 2 as well as the feasibility studies process in evaluating building refurbishment, we will now be able to understand more clearly the thinking processes a building owner goes through before he decides whether to embark on Building Refurbishment.

They are as follows :-

1. Identify various options for physical change within the "low" to "high" strategies
2. Evaluate the practicality and utility of these options and shortlist two to five feasible strategies

3. Carry out economic feasibility studies and further narrow down to one to two economic feasible options.

Chapter 3 will elaborate more on the various Building Refurbishment strategies.

CHAPTER 3

Renew, Re-position, Re-create

Learning objective

- To appreciate how some of the construction technology in Building Refurbishment add value to buildings
- To be aware of how Building Refurbishment plays a part in renewing a building and even a geographical area
- To evaluate how changes could be made to buildings to re-position or re-create the buildings

3.1   Renew

Often as a city progresses its old building stocks faces competition from newer buildings. These old buildings also fall behind in terms of statutory building standards. When the usual cyclical and routine property maintenance does not restore the building value, it's time to consider renewing these buildings with greater overhaul.

What I observed is such building renewal can be carried out at two levels – at the building level or even at the estate level. The building renewal is of course carried out by the building owner whereas the estate or area renewal is often done by the local government or by large private developers or through public private partnerships.

Building Refurbishment can renew a building aesthetically without much structural intervention to the building. Based on my re-interpretation of the David Kincaid (2002) concept (Chapter 2), this is a "medium-low" or "high-low" change. This is done in the form of façade intervention. Often this tends to be for buildings which keep its current use or trade mix without much change.

It could also be in the form of retrofitting the building mechanical and electrical systems to improve its energy efficiency or indoor air quality. This as compared to "re-positioning" and "re-creating" a building seems to suggest no change of use of the building.

Estate Renewal

Estate renewal tends to incorporate some or all of the three Building Refurbishment concepts – renew, re-position, re-create. This is because the scale of the estate renewal is much larger and there is potential to carry out more governmental intervention. A more detailed explanation of estate renewal is beyond the scope of this book. The parameters of describing estate renewal would also involve disciplines such as architectural design, urban planning, government policy, infrastructure investment etc.

A good example of estate renewal is the case of Bugis Junction in Singapore. Originally an area filled with rows of pre-war shophouses, the area is acquired by the government and later sold as part of a land sales. The streets within the area are then permanently pedestrianized. Long span over-roofing spans between these two rows of shophouses to create a new shopping experience previously not available. The private developer who bought the land developed a 5 star hotel, an office block and a mall with direct connectivity to an underground MRT. See Figure 3.2.

3.2   What is re-facade?

Renewing a building through re-façade usually involves re-cladding or over-cladding. This depends on the building owner's intention and existing building performance. The general idea is:-

Re-cladding -   to replace the existing external wall system of a building with a completely new system

Over-cladding-   to install a new cladding system **over** the existing external wall system of a building

The objectives of re-cladding are to:-

- reduce the heat losses through the façade and to meet modern thermal regulations
- improve the appearance of a building
- arrest the deterioration of the existing structure or façade including water leakage
- reducing the external noise level

As such the advantages for re-cladding are:-

- saving in energy bill due to improved insulation
- increasing in the effective lifespan of the building
- improving the appearance and overall amenity of the building and therefore increasing the rental value of the building
- It is more cost effective than demolition and redevelop
- It is a substantial reduction in future maintenance cost in façade maintenance

Some of the major concerns in re-cladding work are:-

- Disturbance to existing occupants during construction - drilling noise and the movement of construction workers within the building
- Whether there is an over-loading of foundations with additional load from the new cladding which can be mitigated with light-weight aluminum façade system
- The need to ensure that the new façade system takes care of all the possible movements for example wind load and thermal movement

In certain cases instead of re-cladding the building owner may choose to carry out over-cladding instead. This method retains the old façade and covers it with a new façade.

3.3   Over-roofing

In an attempt to introduce more thermal comfort (in a tropical country) or weather resistance, building owners may enclose an open space within a building. This comes in the form of over-roofing which usually comes in the form of long span sky roof or glazing.

Over-roofing differs from re-roofing. Re-roofing usually refers to the stripping and laying of new flat roof or retiling of the pitched roof as the original water-proofing may have deteriorated. Over-roofing usually refers to erecting a new roofing system. This can be over an existing empty space of a building for example its atrium space or it could be on top of the building above the existing roof system. It may or may not part of the vertical extension of the building.

Some of the reasons for over-roofing are:-

- rectification of long term roof failure – new roof acts as additional protection layer against the external elements
- improve weather tightness
- aesthetics reasons

- improve thermal insulation of the roof
- reduction in maintenance costs

Some of the advantages of over-roofing are:-

- Increase in usable floor area
- enhances appearance of building
- improves the rainwater disposal efficiency and weather resistance
- extends building life and improves thermal performance
- improves the marketability of the building
- avoids demolition and disposal of existing roof system

See Figure 3.1 and 3.2 for examples on building re-façade and over-roofing

Figure 3.1 – Industrial building re-facade

25 Jun 2014 – Cambridge Industrial REIT carrying out re-facade of one of its industrial building

Figure 3.2 – Bugis Junction in Singapore Over-roofing to create usable commercial space

Roof glazing between two rows of shophouses to create usable commercial space with InterContinental Hotel in the background

3.4   Re-position

Re-positioning is a value creation strategy by commercial building owners to increase its rental income for better building financial performance

Re-positioning is a value creation strategy by commercial building owners to increase its rental income for better building financial performance. A typical example is a shopping mall which is facing obsolescence or suffers from the exit of its major anchor tenant. It could either try to renew itself or find a replacement anchor tenant or re-position itself.

Depending on the location of the mall, the owner could consider re-positioning the mall to premium outlet mall, outlet mall, super luxury mall, theme mall, street fashion mall etc. The same can happen to other property types e.g. office owner upgrading their building to be a Grade A office or hoteliers re-branding the hotel to suit a different user profile etc. I observed however at least in the case of Singapore that re-positioning tend to occur more frequently for malls within a very competitive area e.g. Orchard Road.

Re-positioning of malls is also happening in the sub-urban area as long as there is a strong motivation and competitive forces driving it. In the case of a mall called "IMM" located at the western part of Singapore called Jurong East, it has undergone two major changes since CapitaMall Trust bought over it in 2003. A major Building Refurbishment was carried out over 2003-2004 as part of its asset enhancement initiative "de-canting" some of its gross floor area for higher and more productive use. Capitalizing on what is already a strong positioning as the destination for furniture and bridal arrangement shopping, CapitaMall further added more shopping elements e.g. boutique and restaurants.

Ten years later with the introduction of the Singapore government masterplan concept of "Lakeside" district to turn Jurong East into one of the biggest commercial district outside its CBD, two major malls were added nearby IMM since 2013 – Capitaland's Westgate and Lend Lease's Jem. With more intense competition IMM undergone yet another Building Refurbishment over 2013-2014 to re-position itself into "The Largest Outlet Mall".

Figure 3.3 – IMM in Singapore

Yet another example is a mall called "Chinatown Point" located at the fringe of Singapore's Chinatown. After the retail portion of the complex is acquired by Perennial Real Estate in 2010, it has re-positioned itself into a lifestyle family mall with a major Building Refurbishment. Almost half of the mall original structure was modified to accommodate a new layout. Its façade is completely changed. More strategically Perennial Real Estate has sized on the opportunity to connect to a new MRT line called "Downtown Line" at its "Chinatown" station. This not only improves shopper flow but also increases its visibility to consumers. See Figure 3.4

Re-positioning of a building can arise from the owner's desire to enhance or increase the building profile. This is a case in point that Building Refurbishment need not arise from maintenance related issues. It could be a case of building owners wanting to compete better or do not wish to suffer any drop in rental income level. In the case of IMM it only takes CapitaMall about ten years to carry out another round of Building Refurbishment. During those ten years the external environment has changed which prompted the owner to re-look into the mall positioning.

Re-positioning of mall is to certain extent related to the leasing practice of the country. In Singapore and in many parts of Asia, commercial tenancy typically does not go beyond six to nine years. Each lease term is typically three years with an option to renew for another one or two more terms. What this means is that while the marketing manager may have done an excellent job in the beginning when a new mall opens in terms of retail mix, the mall may undergo several changes in tenant mix after every approximately three years. Hence after about six to nine years, the mall retail mix may not be ideal and aligned with its initial intended positioning.

Figure 3.4 – Chinatown Point in Singapore. Downward
extension to connect to a new MRT train entrance as part of
its connectivity strategy in its Building Refurbishment

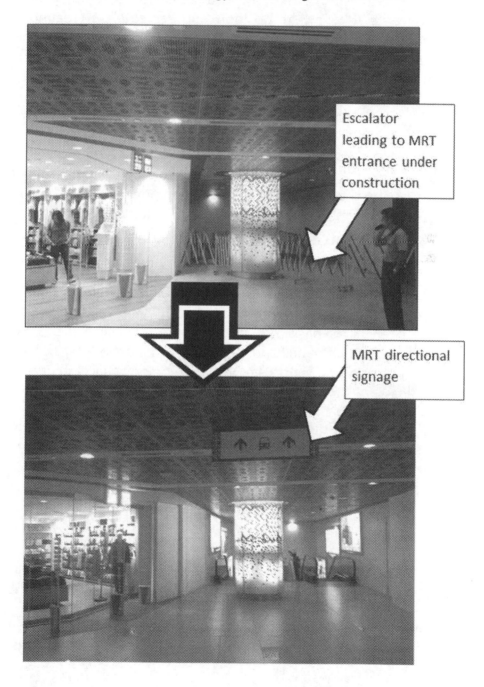

3.5 Re-create

Perhaps the most risky of the three Building Refurbishment concepts – renew, re-position and recreate, re-creating a building typically involves conversion and change of use. It is risky because by adapting the building to suit a completely new use, the owner faces problems in terms of:-

- Whether the existing building structure can be adapted and is not too technically challenging to adapt. This is because every building type has its own typology and so the existing building layout and ceiling height must be changed to suit the new typology.
- Possible site constraints for example downtown
- Regulatory challenge in obtaining approval for change of use

In many cities with growing tourist arrival there are great demands for hotel. In Singapore the tourist arrival has climbed from ten million back in 2008 to more than 15 million in 2013. As such several office buildings are converted into hotel by existing owners or new owners. The obvious typology challenge is that office differs from hotel typology in at least the following:-

- Hotel requires compartmentalizing of the floor to create rooms and requires toilet, sanitary, air-conditioning and electrical services for each room
- Most higher end hotels have generous double or even triple volume ceilings at their lobbies to create grand impression
- Every room needs a view

Another interesting area is the conversion of heritage building. Increasingly we are aware that buildings which have architectural merit or history value should be preserved. The challenge then is to find new uses for these preserved or heritage buildings.

Many of them are converted to hotels, malls, galleries or museums all over the world.

A very good example in Singapore is The Fullerton Hotel located at the heart of the Central Business District next to the Singapore River. What used to be an administrative office for the then colonial British government built in the 1920s and later used by several Singapore government offices and even as a post office, is gloriously restored and converted to a luxurious hotel. Over-roofing is added to what was previously an open courtyard. Its internal structural floors were gutted out to create a generous atrium. This is so that there could also be rooms facing internally in order to maximize revenue. Additional basement has to be built and strict guidelines were adhered to in its façade restoration.

Change of use

As mentioned re-creating a real estate usually requires a change of use. In the regulatory planning control sense, this refers to the change of the building use from one use to another. An example is the converting an office building into a hotel. We will discuss more about the concept of change of use in Chapter 6.

Josh Ng

Figure 3.5 – The Fullerton Hotel Singapore

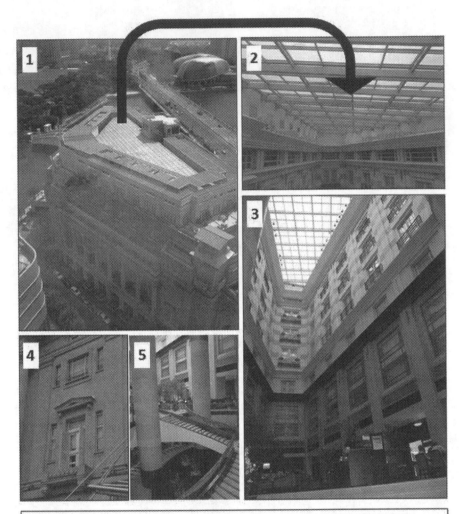

1/2 – Over-roofing is carried to cover the entire atrium which used to be a open courtyard typical of a lot of colonial buildings in the past.
3 – several floor slab is demolished so that a high volume atrium can be created and additional hotel guestroom facing the atrium can be incorporated.
4 – old façade restored to its former glory
5 – a partial downward extension is carried out to create additional ballrooms

3.6   Summary

The following table summarise the possible differences among these three Building Refurbishment concepts.

Building Refurbishment concepts	Renew	Re-position	Re-create
Common practices	Re-façade, interior works, M&E retrofit or a combination of all aspects to improve the building aesthetic and indoor environment	Some façade and also structural intervention to upgrade the building use to serve higher end users while keeping the same building use.	Major structural intervention and some or major façade intervention to accommodate a change of use to the building
Possible examples	Re-façade of old office buildings	Re-positioning of old mall to accommodate new concept	Convert an old heritage building into a hotel
Extent of change of use	Little of no change of use	Possible change of use or no change of use but change of trade or tenant mix	Complete change of use

CHAPTER 4

Creating Value
— Asset Enhancement Strategies

Learning objective

- To relate to the broad Building Refurbishment strategies – renew, re-position, re-create in the context of REITs property portfolio or commercial building owner
- To be able to evaluate the Asset Enhancement Strategies adopted by REITs to boost their property performance and value

4.1 Renew, re-position and re-create in the context of REITs or commercial building owner

A large part of the motivation for carrying out Building Refurbishment for commercial properties is to CREATE VALUE. Commercial building for the purpose of this book refers once again to any building which is earning rental income for the building owner. Hence we are adopting the perspective of how Building Refurbishment INCREASE the rental income of the commercial properties and hence its VALUE.

Chapter 3 outlines the broad Building Refurbishment strategies. All of the three strategies are to increase property value. The extent of the property value increase depends on how effective is the Building Refurbishment.

A large part of the motivation for carrying out Building Refurbishment for commercial properties is to **CREATE VALUE.**

Chapter 2 proposes how these Building Refurbishment should be measured in terms of the extent of intervention to the building façade and structure as well as how to measure the feasibility of such Building Refurbishment projects. With such measurement and analysis we can then measure how effective is the Building Refurbishment and therefore how much VALUE is created.

In the context of REITs or real estate investment trusts, the performance of their properties portfolio is highly tied to the REITs share prices. This indirectly also affects the fee earned by the REITs manager. As a result there is a huge incentive for the REITs manager to boost their properties income. One of the options besides signing higher paying tenant or selling their buildings for a profit is to adopt Asset Enhancement Strategies. Among the few Asset Enhancement Strategies is to renew, re-position or re-create their buildings through Building Refurbishment. The same applies to commercial building owners.

It is however rather broad to summarily describe VALUE CREATION as the result of adopting these three strategies mentioned in Chapter 3. In order to measure VALUE CREATION we need to be more specific by identifying which aspects of the asset enhancement is CREATING VALUE. This chapter will explain the essence of the VALUE CREATION without going too much into the detailed feasibility studies calculation which is best left to investment analysis books.

4.2   Essence of commercial building performance and value

One way to examine the property performance is to consider its value based on the capitalization method which is essentially based on this formula:-

$$\text{Capital Value} = \frac{\text{Annual Net Operating Income}}{\text{Yield}}$$

"Yield" in this case refers to the investor expected rate of return which can be based on the overall investment or just based on the equity invested. While there is a certain norm, there is no fixed "Yield" for any given property or property type. It is also benchmarked against the yield from equity investment instruments, for example, shares and also against debt instruments, for example, government bonds. Rightfully, property yield should fall in between the expected rate of return from shares and bonds.

Even within the whole range of property investment available, there is a range of "Yield" expected from various types of property. A prime downtown office building would have a lower yield than an industrial building. An industrial building may have a lower yield than say a strata titled industrial unit.

Theoretically a yield of a property can also be derived from the net property income a property achieved versus its capital value:-

$$\text{Yeild} = \frac{\text{Annual Net Operating Income}}{\text{Capital Value}}$$

So exactly how do we calculate the annual net operating income for a building? We would need to know the building's:-

- Gross floor area ("GFA")
- Efficiency
- Average rental rate
- Annual operating expenditure

In certain countries, the GFA is based on consultation with the local building council or authorities. In other cases like the case of Singapore it is based on a certain master planning. Such master planning could determine the possible intensification allowed using for example a certain plot ratio. As such, the GFA of a building is the multiplication of the land area with this plot ratio. We should also clarify whether the building GFA includes car-parking and what is the building setback required from the site boundaries. Otherwise, the maximum GFA which can be built is affected.

A building efficiency is the percentage of the GFA which can be used for leasing or generating rental income. The net area that can be used for rental is called the net floor area ("NFA") or leasable floor area ("LFA"). Typically an office building has an efficiency of 90% and that of a mall is 60%. An industrial building can have an efficiency of 100%. The following further illustrate the calculation of NFA of a mall in Singapore:-

GFA	Efficiency	NFA
10,000sqm	x 60%	= 6,000sqm
The maximum built up space a mall can have. This does not include car-parking	The other 40% is distributed among public areas and non-productive space e.g. lobby, corridor, atrium, plant room etc	Leasable area within the building

The most interesting aspect of marketing a commercial building is that there are in fact several different types of rental rate achievable. This is due to the different location within the building and also the timing of the transaction. Hence in order to do a quick calculation we could adopt the average building rental rate.

A building operating expenditure consists primarily of its maintenance cost, utility cost, insurance and property tax.

With the calculation of the NFA, we could find the building annual gross rental income by carrying out this calculation:-

NFA	x Average rental rate	x 12 months	x (1 – vacancy rate)	= Annual gross rental income
For example 6,000sqm	x $10 per sqm	x 12 months	x (1- 10% vacancy)	= $648,000

4.3   Four specific Asset Enhancement Strategies to CREATE VALUE

With the understanding of Chapter 4.2, it then follows that if any of the following is carried out, we can CREATE VALUE:-

- Increase GFA we increase NFA (assuming the same efficiency) we increase net operating income ("NOI") we increase property value of a commercial building based on the capitalization method :-

$$\text{Capital Value} = \frac{\text{Annual Net Operating Income}}{\text{Yield}}$$

- Increase the efficiency we increase NFA (assuming the same GFA) we increase NOI we increase property value (again!)

- Increase average rental rate we increase gross income (assuming same GFA and efficiency) we increase NOI and we also increase property value!
- Lower the operating expenditure we increase NOI and again increase property value.

Strategy 1 - Increase GFA

GFA can be increased if additional GFA is given to the building owner arising from a change in local building regulations or code. Or it could be bought by the building owner through the payment of development charges. With these additional GFA the building owner would usually extend the building either vertically upwards if it has not reached its height control limits. Or the building owner could extend the building horizontally if the site permits after considering the building setback.

We are assuming that these additional GFA are legally constructed and permitted by the local building council or authorities. This is because as explained in Chapter 2 there are technical considerations which if not observed could lead to fatal consequences. As in the case of a Bangladesh garment factory which collapsed in Apr 2013. What was originally designed to be only four stories was added on with an additional two more stories illegally. In addition the garment factory within the building was overloaded with too many people. As a result of over-loading of dead load and live load the building gave way and caused the death of hundreds of people.

An example which sees an increase of GFA for an old development in Singapore is "Raffles City" located in heart of its civic district. Raffles City is a mixed development with the now Fairmont Hotel, the Raffles City Convention Centre and Raffles City Shopping Centre. It has direct connection to the Singapore MRT interchange station "City Hall" which connects the East-West and North-South line. "Raffles City" was built since 1986-87. With the completion of yet another MRT line

"Circle Line" near Raffles City in 2010, connectivity to Raffles City is created to link to a Circle Line MRT station called "Esplanade". In the process of this connectivity additional GFA is granted to Raffles City. CapitaCommercial Trust and CapitaMall Trust the manager of Raffles City Shopping Centre took the opportunity to revamp its basement retail offering through a major Building Refurbishment. CapitaCommercial Trust and CapitaMall Trust also increased the rental rate of Raffles City basement level and improved its efficiency. Other initiatives included the creation is a brand new retail section within what was previously the mall's atrium.

Strategy 2 - Improve efficiency

Not every country would stipulate the required efficiency to be achieved by every building owner. The minimum requirement should be that the building is safe and functional for its purpose. What it means to be "safe" primarily focuses on the compliance of the building design with the local fire code such that the necessary fire protection and fighting measures are not compromised. For example the fire escape route should be of a certain spatial standard. The building should be installed with fire sprinkler if it is of a certain height. The fire escape staircase should be fire-rated etc. Of course there are other technical consideration and code compliance as well for a building design which is beyond the scope of this book.

What is equally important also is that the building should be fit for its purpose. The spatial layout and design should suit its use. This is what architect calls the "typology" of a building. One of the reasons why a mall has a lower efficiency than say an office building is because it usually requires a large atrium space to generate activities and create promotion for the mall.

If a building owner could convert unproductive space which does not earn any single cent to a leasable space without compromising the local code compliance especially the fire code, then we CREATE VALUE. Most mall owners typically include push carts to boost rental revenue. This is not effective in creating value as the increase in NOI is marginal. What would be an effective increase in efficiency is when the building owner re-aligns the layout or re-designs the circulation such that the permanent NFA is increased.

A good case in point is the acquisition by CapitaMall Trust of the then "Iluma" a mall just opposite Bugis Junction - one of the many malls managed by CapitaMall Trust for SGD295 million in 2011. "Iluma" which is rebranded as "Bugis+" has an efficiency of 63% which according to CapitaMall is below its portfolio average of 68%. Instantly there is some possible value extraction by CapitaMall Trust through Building Refurbishment. This translate indirectly to an approximately 4.5% increase in property value assuming a 10% outgoing. It was a strategic move by CapitaMall as "Bugis+" is now connected directly to Bugis Junction and enjoys greater footfall and creates a larger retail footprint and CapitaMall presence for that area. Other asset enhancement strategies deployed at that time include increasing the rental rate and improve the retail mix of Bugis+ upon the expiry of its prime level 1 and 2 leases. See Figure 4.1.

Figure 4.1 – CapitaMall Trust increases the efficiency of "Bugis+"

15 May 2009 – The then Iluma without the bridge to Bugis Junction. Iluma is later on sold to Capitaland in 2011	22 Dec 2014 – Bugis+ now with direct bridge connection to Bugis Junction. Bugis Village managed by CapitaCommercial Trust is also nearby

Strategy 3 - Increase rental rate

If a building owner faces the constraints of fixed GFA and efficiency, there is very little way to manipulate the NFA. Then the next best move is to "re-position" the building for higher rental rate signing. This could come in one or more of the following situation:-

If a building owner faces the constraints of fixed GFA and efficiency, there is very little way to manipulate the NFA. Then the next best move is to "re-position" the building for higher rental rate signing.

- Office building – "renew" the building by re-cladding its façade. With the new look and possibly renovation to its interior, for example, the lobby and toilets the office building owner creates a better workplace environment. He could then possibly increase the rental rate (usually marginally higher).
- Malls – The mall owner "re-position" the mall to cater to higher value tenants for example luxury products retailer to attract higher paying shoppers. Without changing the NFA the mall owner increases the mall value by increasing (substantially) the rental rate. But of course the mall owner needs to carry out careful economic feasibility to ensure that the mall re-positioning is sustainable.
- Office building – previously the entrance level of the office building at Level 1 does not earn the owner any single cent. By converting Level 1 and sometimes even Level 2 into retail especially cafes and restaurant or convenience store, there is now a multiple increase in rental rate for those NFA within Level 1 and 2.
- Mixed hotel and retail development – typically the lower levels of the hotel has some boutique and retail shops which caters to tourists and hotel guests. By converting

a larger part of the lower levels into a lifestyle mall and shifting the hotel concierge and welcome lobby to say Level 3, the hotel building increase the rental rate of what was previously low rental rate or dead rental area.

A good example of an increase in rental rate as part of the asset enhancement strategy is the Building Refurbishment carried out by CapitaMall Trust for Plaza Singapura and The Atrium. These are two commercial buildings located at the "Dhoby Ghaut" MRT station located at the corner of Singapore Orchard Road.

Plaza Singapura is already owned by CapitaMall Trust and The Atrium is bought by CapitaMall Trust for S$839.8 million in 2008. This acquisition presented CapitaMall Trust a unique opportunity to create a long presence along Orchard Road. Hence both buildings are merged. Specifically they are merged and connected at Level 1, 3 and 4. These are the levels where The Atrium was converted from either non-productive atrium space or lower yielding office space into retail space. A new façade now wraps around the perimeter of the two buildings to create an impression of an integrated development. See Figure 4.2.

Strategy 4 – Reduce operating expenditure

The operating expenditure of a building is primarily reduced by deploying more energy efficient equipment and practices. The major equipment to tackle would be the air-conditioning equipment (in the case of a tropical country like Singapore) e.g. chiller, air handling units etc.

Another area to look into is the re-façade or over-façade of the building to reduce the heat load of the building. As a result the air-conditioning energy and hence cost of the building is reduced. The use of artificial lighting near the façade, assuming it is a glass façade, is also reduced.

However Strategy 4 – reducing operating expenditure – is probably the least effective in creating value as its impact is not as substantial as Strategy 1,2 and 3. This is because a typical operating expenditure of a commercial building forms only about 10-15% of its gross income. As such a 10% saving in operating expenditure for example, only increases about 1% of the commercial building's net operating income.

If we consider the fact that most of the initiatives for reducing operating expenditure focus on implementing energy efficiency program for the building, their impact on the building real estate value is minimal. This is because such initiatives form only a part of the operating expenditure. If for instance the building utility cost is 40% of the operating expenditure, a 10% reduction in energy cost contributes only 4% in operating expenditure saving. If the operating expenditure is 10% of the building gross income, then a 4% reduction in operating expenditure contributes a 0.4% increase in net operating income only. This could represent an 8% increase in capital value if we adopt a 5% yield. There are also other benefits such as recognition for being a green building and better indoor environment and therefore greater user satisfaction etc.

4.4   Considerations before carrying out Asset Enhancement Strategies

However in order to carry out these asset enhancement strategies asset manager should consider the new positioning of the building and hence its possible physical change to accommodate the new positioning. This involves a multi-disciplinary approach involving the architect, marketing department and structural and M&E engineer. Asset enhancement of a commercial building is more than just bringing in new tenants. The other salient points to consider during asset enhancement are:-

• New image and hence possible re-façade work

- Circulation of user, shoppers, pedestrian and cars traffic as well as carpark design. Positioning of elevators, travelators and staircase
- Re-design and distribution of M&E services
- Structural integrity of the building while undergoing refurbishment
- Ceiling height and building height constraints etc
- How to maintain the property income while undergoing refurbishment without too much impact on tenant business and shopper traffic
- How to retain tenants and not breach any tenancy agreement

Essentially all aspects of the refurbishment regulation related to construction as mentioned in other chapters in this book are also involved. See Chapter 6 and Chapter 7.

4.5 Summary

A large part of the motivation for carrying out Building Refurbishment for commercial properties is to CREATE VALUE. There are 4 specific asset enhancement strategies:-

Strategy 1 – increase the building GFA
Strategy 2 – increase the efficiency in the use of GFA
Strategy 3 – increase the rental rate of the commercial building
Strategy 4 – reduce the building operating expenditure

Often asset enhancement of a commercial building involves more than one strategy. The least effective of the four strategies is Strategy 4.

Figure 4.2 – CapitaMall Trust increases the rental rate of The Atrium

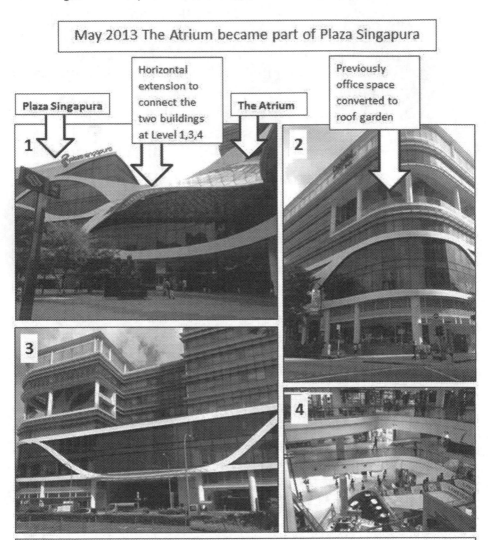

May 2013 The Atrium became part of Plaza Singapura

Plaza Singapura

Horizontal extension to connect the two buildings at Level 1,3,4

The Atrium

Previously office space converted to roof garden

1/2/3 – a new façade wraps around the two building – Plaza Singapura and The Atrium to integrate them both.
2 – GFA from what was previously office space is used to create retail space at Level 1,3,4
3 – Level 3 , 4 with a slightly darker façade is retail space converted from office space
4 – New retail space. Rental rate is increased from less than S$0-10psf to now S$10- 20psf

CHAPTER 5

Building Refurbishment And Competition — Singapore Case Studies

5.1   My hypothesis

My hypothesis is that the trigger for a commercial Building Refurbishment could arise more from the immediate competitive environment rather than from other factors. This is especially so within a highly concentrated commercial zone.

Traditionally Building Refurbishment arises from building obsolescence and redundancy as explained in Section 1.6 of this book. However we should note that there are other motivations which trigger the refurbishment which are also explained in my Chapter 1:-

- the change in the political, economic, social or technological environment
- changes in the way we design buildings and the need to update the buildings to the latest designs
- financial returns expected from refurbishment
- the need to have a new building sooner as its lease is very short
- competition
- the government restriction on conserved buildings

One of the major factors which trigger a lot of commercial Building Refurbishment within high commercial building concentration areas is perhaps competition. I will attempt to illustrate the relationship between the intensity of existing commercial Building Refurbishment and perceived threats from newly completed commercial buildings by examining two areas in Singapore:-

- Marina Bay area
- Orchard Road

We examine the following factors in an attempt to examine the relationship between competition and intensity of commercial Building Refurbishment:-

- the distance from the refurbished commercial building from the latest brand new commercial development
- the percentage of the refurbishment cost versus the cost of constructing the latest brand new commercial development

Refer to Charts 5.1 and 5.2 for better visualization and understanding.

5.2   Marina Bay area

For the purpose of this study, I will focus primarily only on shopping malls or office buildings with major retail space or hotel with major retail space.

When we look at the Marina Bay area of Singapore, one of the new major competitors within this area is the Marina Bay Sands Integrated Resort. It was completed and opened on 27 April 2010 and cost a massive S$7b. Marina Bay Sands has a massive 570,000 square metre GFA which comprises luxury high end retail space, more 2,500 hotel rooms, convention centre for 45,000 people and other unique features e.g. the Skypark,

Infinity Pool, Art Science Museum etc. A whole new service standard and customer experience was introduced with the opening of Marina Bay Sands.

It is little wonder that the neighbours of Marina Bay Sands have responded pro-actively by refurbishing their buildings. The most notable is the phased refurbishment of Suntec City S$410m revamp from 2009 to 2014. The phased refurbishment of Marina Square Shopping Mall – Phase 1 S$15m has completed and opened in July 2013 and Phase 2 S$80m new 200,000 square feet wing will be opened in 1st quarter 2015.

Another major commercial building in the vicinity – Millenia Walk – also has refurbishment in 2009 and 2010 but was of smaller scale as compared to Suntec City and Marina Square. The refurbishment of Millenia Walk in 2009 was to sub-divide the internal layout in response to the re-sizing of Harvey Norman - a major Australian furniture and electrical store. Subsequently its 2010's refurbishment was more in response to the opening of a new MRT Circle Line "Promenade" station as well as incorporating the re-entry of Parco a Japanese departmental store. Parco has since vacated from Millenia Walk in 2014 and new concept and stores will be revealed in its place.

Further away at the Bugis precinct in the vicinity of "Bugis" MRT station, CapitaMall Trust took back about 70,000 square feet of retail space from their anchor tenant BHG department store. These space were converted to specialty store which fetches higher rental rate. Efficiency is also improved with some straightening of the circulation. The asset enhancement is completed in third quarter 2014 at the cost of SGD35 million.

The asset enhancement initiative at Bugis Junction ties in very nicely with another of CapitaMall Trust's mall at "Bugis+". Originally called "Iluma" by the previous owner and not connected to "Bugis Junction", CapitaMall Trust connected "Bugis+" directly to "Bugis Junction" to create a critical mass of

600,000 square feet of retail space. "Bugis+" asset enhancement to improve its building efficiency by 5% and redesign of tenant mix cost SGD38 million. It was completed in Jul 2012.

A Straits Times article on 2 Sep 2011 reported that CityLink Mall an underground mall linking Raffles City and Suntec City / Suntec Convention Centre, spent SGD10 million to make over the underground mall. It is renewed with brighter finishes and new directional signage. It is reported that its refurbishment is completed in end 2012.

Not too far away from CityLink Mall, another prime asset owned by Perennial Real Estate called "CHIJMES" undergone a Building Refurbishment costing SGD45 million. It was completed in 2014. According to Perennial "the changes are not just physical ... also upmarket...". This represents that there is re-positioning of the mall. CHIJMES is a conserved historical building converted into retail use located in the heart of Singapore's Civic District.

A bit further West of Marina Bay Sands and two MRT stations away, "One Raffles Place", a Grade A office development located at "Raffles Place" MRT. About 95,000 square feet of retail space in its retail podium is refurbished and re-positioned for higher use. Brands such as H&M and Uniqlo are introduced. No refurbishment cost is reported and it was completed in May 2014.

See Chart 5.1 for a summary of the Building Refurbishment projects mentioned above. Total estimated Building Refurbishment cost over the last five years is S$713m which represents about 9% of Marina Bay Sands development cost.

Chart 5.1 – A measure of the intensity of Building
Refurbishment projects in Marina Bay Sands vicinity.

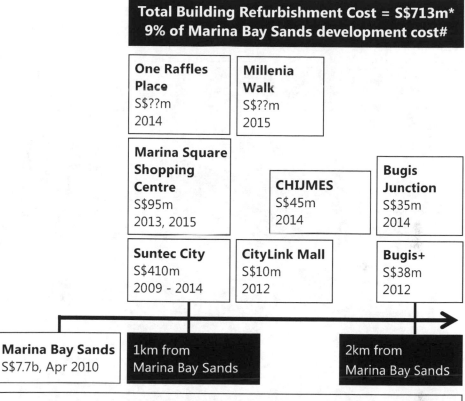

| Total Building Refurbishment Cost = S$713m* |
| 9% of Marina Bay Sands development cost# |

One Raffles Place
S$??m
2014

Millenia Walk
S$??m
2015

Marina Square Shopping Centre
S$95m
2013, 2015

CHIJMES
S$45m
2014

Bugis Junction
S$35m
2014

Suntec City
S$410m
2009 - 2014

CityLink Mall
S$10m
2012

Bugis+
S$38m
2012

Marina Bay Sands
S$7.7b, Apr 2010

1km from Marina Bay Sands

2km from Marina Bay Sands

*assuming S$40m spent for One Raffles Place and for Millenia Walk
Marina Bay Sands S$7.7b development cost includes land cost,
consultant fee, construction cost, furnishing cost etc.. Building
Refurbishment cost excludes these.

MARINA BAY AREA

Figure 5.1 – Re-facade of Suntec Convention Centre

23 Dec 2012 – Suntec Convention Centre – re-façade to create a new image
and retail mall at Level 1-2 and new configuration for convention centre

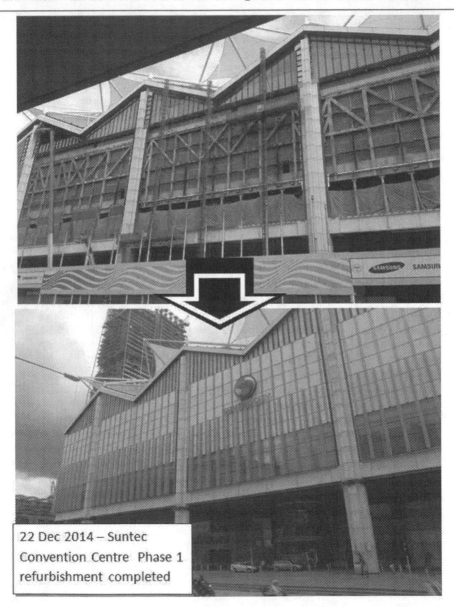

22 Dec 2014 – Suntec
Convention Centre Phase 1
refurbishment completed

Figure 5.2 – Re-configuration of Suntec Convention Centre
to Incorporate LED screen and more retail shops

28 Jun 2009 Suntec Convention Centre entrance then
versus 29 Oct 2014 current design

Josh Ng

Figure 5.3 – Increasing more productive NLA after the exit of Carrefour

29 Apr 2012 Carrefour moving out of Suntec City versus 29 Oct 2014 the new tenant- mix after its Phase 2 refurbishment

Figure 5.4 – Changes in Millenia Walk

12 July 2009 – Millenia Walk – carrying out work to sub-divide upper floor upon re-sizing of anchor tenant Harvey Norman.

14 Mar 2013 - Millenia Walk – Picture shows the anchor tenant Parco.
29 Oct 2014 – Exit of Parco from Millenia Walk

Figure 5.5 – Asset enhancement in Marina Square
Shopping Centre – Phase 1 and Phase 2

5.3 Orchard Road area

Orchard Road Singapore is one of the most famous shopping belts in the region. It has become more of a regional catchment, attracting tourists internationally and from the region as well as locals all over Singapore. Several foreign retail brands establish its presence in Singapore by first setting up its first store along Orchard Road.

Since 2009 the retail landscape in Singapore Orchard Road has changed with the arrival of three major shopping malls:-

- ION Orchard owned by Capitaland and Sun Hung Kai Properties joint venture
- 313 Somerset owned and developed by Lend Lease

- Orchard Central owned and developed by Far East Organisation

ION Orchard is located right on top of the Orchard MRT and has a luxury high end residential tower as well. As for 313 Somerset and Orchard Central, they are connected to the Somerset MRT. Both are along Orchard Road.

Incidentally the incumbent shopping magnets – Paragon and Takashimaya Departmental Store at Ngee Ann City - are located between these two MRT stations. Other major commercial buildings prior to the arrival of these three new commercial buildings are Wisma Atria, Tangs, Centrepoint.

As such it is not too difficult to understand the competitive environment facing all the major commercial buildings along Orchard Road. Chart 5.2 maps:-

- the frequency of Building Refurbishment occurrence after 2009
- the amount of refurbishment cost spent and
- the proximity of these refurbishments to the new developments

Based on Chart 5.2, we could see that there seems to be a relationship between the proximity of the existing commercial buildings to the new commercial developments and the likelihood of triggering a Building Refurbishment.

A total of approximately almost S$1 billion is spent or will be spent from 2009 to 2017. The majority of these Building Refurbishment projects are between Orchard MRT and Somerset MRT. Their total refurbishment cost is estimated to be S$791 million which represents about 80% of the total refurbishment done along Orchard Road.

Chart 5.2 – A measure of the intensity of Building
Refurbishment projects along Orchard Road

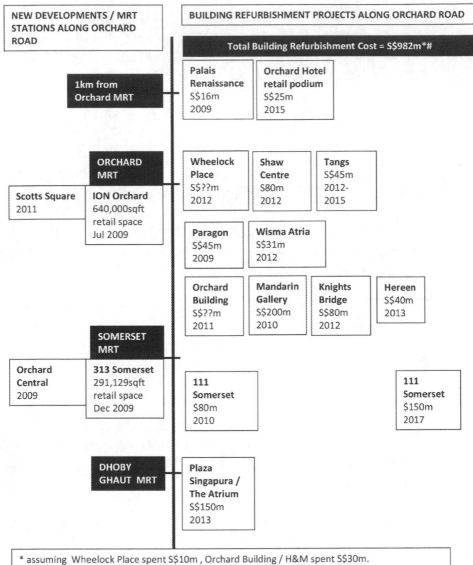

* assuming Wheelock Place spent S$10m , Orchard Building / H&M spent S$30m.
# development cost of the new developments along Orchard Road is not available

ORCHARD ROAD AREA

Figure 5.6 – Shaw Centre asset enhancement to
integrate Shaw Centre and Shaw House

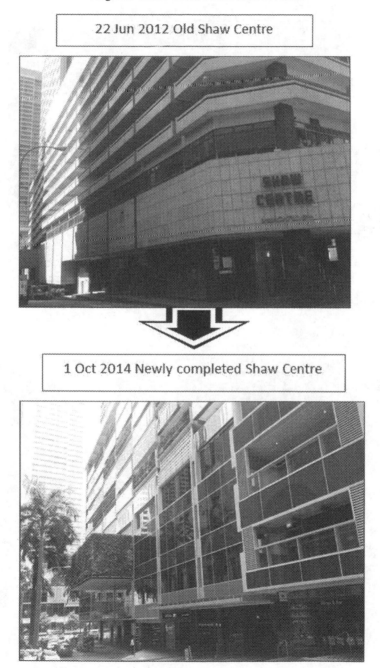

Josh Ng

Figure 5.7 – Wisma Atria second major refurbishment

2 Jun 2009 – Wisma Atria version 2 versus 2014 Wisma Atria version 3

22 Dec 2014 – Wisma Atria version 3

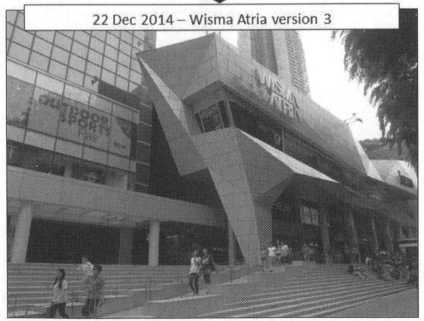

Figure 5.8 – Refurbishment of Orchard Building to accommodate
H&M four stories flagship store at Orchard Road

11 Jun 2009 - Orchard
Building - Before its lower 3
levels were converted to
H&M Singapore first flagship
store

22 Dec 2014 - Orchard
Building with now 4 levels of
H&M

Josh Ng

Figure 5.9 – Mandarin Gallery S$200m refurbishment

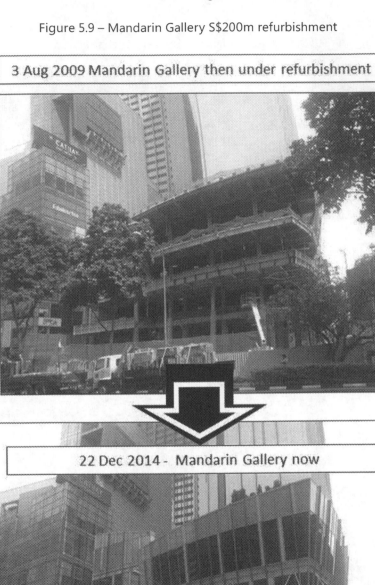

Figure 5.10 – Park Hotel S$80m refurbishment which
includes both the hotel and retail portion

2 Jun 2009 – New Park Hotel then versus 2014 the
re-designed New Park Hotel with a more trendy
retail area at Level 1-2

22 Dec 2014 – New
Park Hotel now

Figure 5.11 – Tripleone Somerset asset enhancement by Pacific Star in 2009

2 June 2009 – 111 Somerset refurbishing level 1 to 3 to convert space to retail use.

6 Nov 2009 – 111 Somerset level 1 to 3 retail conversion near completion.

5.4   Summary

There seems to be a relationship between the proximity of the existing commercial building and new commercial development and the likelihood of triggering Building Refurbishment for the existing commercial building. However more research and studies are required to validate the hypothesis. Other factors could include:-

- proximity of infrastructure e.g. the MRT station
- the road network
- government incentives
- the amount of financing available to building owners
- the ownership structure – strata-titled buildings tend not to have any major refurbishment

There could be a relationship between the scales of the Building Refurbishment for existing commercial buildings in relation to the size of the new commercial development. However there is insufficient data and information to investigate such relationship for now.

We should also note that there were also numerous hotel refurbishments in Singapore within the same period arising from the same reason – competitions.

I will attempt to cover more details of these case studies and other types of building refurbishment in my subsequent book.

CHAPTER 6

The Impact of Regulatory Requirements

Learning Objectives

- To briefly explain the various types of government regulations impacting Building Refurbishment
- To identify the challenging situations for Building Refurbishment to comply with government regulations
- To appreciate how in particular planning control, change of use and conservation regulations impact Building Refurbishment.

6.1   Introduction

Building refurbishment being a construction activity is subjected to numerous government regulations. It is required to comply with regulatory codes and industry practices. Building owners who are well versed with such compliance would overcome the most difficult process of building refurbishment process – the construction activity - and enjoy the fruit of his labour with a brand new and marketable space.

As the compliance with government regulations in Building Refurbishment is a complicated matter which requires professional help, it is best managed by professionals. Broadly

Building Refurbishments just like the construction of new buildings is regulated with the following:-

Type of government regulation	Description of the likely scope of the regulation	Professional engaged to assist in handling such regulations	At what stage of the building life would the building be most regulated by the regulations?
• Fire protection and fighting	Fire code which specify the design of passive and active fire fighting measures	• Fire Engineer • Architect • M&E Engineer	• Design • Construction • Use/ Maintenance
• Building design	Building code which specify the minimum habitable standard in terms of floor loading, ceiling height, lighting level, accessibility, thermal comfort level etc	• Architect • Structural Engineer • M&E Engineer	• Design • Construction
• Planning control	Planning regulations which prescribe the building use, maximum gross floor area, building form and height, setback, carparking, change of use, conservation guildelines etc	• Architect • Façade designer/ Engineer • Urban Planner	• Design

One other regulation which is gaining momentum and generally accepted is the regulations on "green" building and "green" design.

If these regulatory requirements affecting Building Refurbishment is handled by professionals, then would the building owners still need to worry? The answer is "yes". This is because the building owners would still need to make decisions whenever there is any trade-off proposed or recommended by the professionals. This is especially since Building Refurbishment involves "live" building and the building owner should know the building better.

Referring back to Chapter 2 to 4, we talked about the thinking process a building owner goes through before deciding on a Building Refurbishment scheme. Upon deciding on a scheme, the building professionals are engaged for the next step – producing detailed design and procuring a contractor. This is when the next two challenges begin.

First of all, any major Building Refurbishment design would need to comply with regulatory requirements. The challenge most of the time is that the existing buildings were often built many years ago. As such they have not kept up with the development of the regulatory codes which may have become more stringent invariably. We will explore this challenge in the next section.

The second challenge is the project management of the Building Refurbishment. What is unique sometimes for Building Refurbishment projects is that the existing buildings may have existing users or tenants while the Building Refurbishment is going on. I call such buildings "live" building. Now even if there are no existing users or tenants within the building, there are other technical issues which set Building Refurbishment apart. For example the protection of existing structure, underpinning of building,

What is unique sometimes for Building Refurbishment projects is that the existing buildings may have existing users or tenants while the Building Refurbishment is going on. I call such buildings "live" building.

conservation issues etc. We will discuss these challenges in Chapter 7.

6.2 Regulatory requirements and building refurbishment

In all Building Refurbishment there are a few major regulatory compliance required as follows:-

Fire Code

Compliance with the fire code is paramount as it concerns life and death for the building occupants and users. A building without the appropriate fire code compliance will also not be able to obtain its occupation permit upon completion of its refurbishment from the local building authorities and hence rendered it not usable. It is however easier said than done as older buildings generally have not kept up with the latest fire code development.

Generally we could classify the fire code compliance into either active fire protection or passive. Active fire protection refers to the use of appropriate fire-fighting mechanism that would either suppress the fire or extract the smoke generated. A lot of injuries and death in a fire arises from the inhalation of smoke rather than being actually burnt.

Usually we should see the following active fire protection features in any buildings:-

- Fire sprinkler (for building more than a certain height)
- Mechanical smoke extraction (for building more than a certain height)
- Fire extinguisher
- Hose reel
- Fire hose

In addition to the active fire-fighting features there are also accompanying monitoring or supporting systems/ equipment:-

- Smoke detectors (which would activate the mechanical smoke extractor)
- Heat detectors
- Dry or wet risers (for fight fighters to connect the water supply to the higher floors)
- Fire alarm
- Fire alarm panel
- Public address system
- Call point

Passive fire protection refers to the use of structural elements to contain fire rather than to fight fire. This is called the fire compartmentalization concept. In another words the walls, structural floors or ceiling as well as the doors or windows must have a certain fire proofing capability up to a certain hours called fire rating. It would make sense that for those part of the building involving fire evacuation there must be at least 1hour fire rating or such other fire rating dictated by the fire code.

While this compartmentalization concept seems sound, it can be compromised whenever there is penetration through the wall or floor because of the provision of building services e.g. air conditioning ducts, electrical risers, water discharge pipes etc. Hence the fire code also stipulates the fire stop measures for such wall and floor penetrations.

One of the most essential aspects of fire safety is to be able to evacuate from the building within an hour or so. In order to do so the local fire code should have stipulated certain dimensioning and distance for the following:-

- travel distance from any part of the building to the nearest fire escape staircase

- width of the corridor for evacuation, fire door leading to fire escape staircase and staircase
- height of staircase and corridor (minimum is 2m but not at all parts of the evacuation route)

In addition there are also a few issues to consider:-

- Occupancy load of the floor
- Number of fire escape staircase
- Ventilation

Challenges in complying with fire code for building refurbishment

One major issue in Building Refurbishment is the updating of the fire protection measures and design of an old building. Such "old" buildings could be as young as only 20 years old. The issue is such old buildings are certified usable based on the fire code at the time of its completion. However fire code could have progressed and developed over the years adding more stringent measures and requirements.

The implication for Building Refurbishment is

- addition site space may be required outside the building for fire engine access (if applicable)
- additional physical building space is required for riser, installation of active fire protection equipment e.g. fire extinguisher, hose reel etc. This may involves coring through the floor for penetration of the risers or pipes etc.
- installation of additional fire-fighting water tank

Another Building Refurbishment scenario which requires drastic changes to the building fire protection design is when a "lower" building use, for example, a school is converted to a "higher" use, e.g. office or retail such as food outlets. We would need to "intensify" the fire protection installations because previously the building has less enclosed space and lower occupancy load as compared to the now "higher" use.

Conserved and preserved buildings especially may warrant a closer look as to how it could comply with the latest fire code during a Building Refurbishment. This is because usually non-typical building material and space dimensions are found in such places. For example, a shophouse floor is usually made of timber and so is its staircase. In such instances, the latest fire code may require the shophouse restoration to use fire retardant paint underneath the timber floor or fire proof boxing up on the underside of the floor.

Yet another challenge is when a Building Refurbishment scheme is implemented only for a part of the existing building. In this case, that part of the building would have to be updated with the latest fire code. Yet, other parts of the existing building which are not affected are still based on the old fire code. This may pose a problem as the new fire-fighting system has to be integrated back to the old system. While it is not a major issue, the inconsistency may cause some confusion to building management staff.

<u>Building Code</u>

Every building must provide circulation space in the form of staircase, corridor, lift lobby etc. and must have sufficient floor loading for each specific use. For example, the floor loading of an office space is 5KN/ m^2. This is the nature of building control which prescribes a minimum habitation standard. It is usually done through imposing several professional code of practice or local standards. Building code generally governs:-

- habitatable space dimensioning for example there could be requirement for minimum ceiling height.
- circulation design – staircase, lifts, ramps etc.
- floor loading capacity of various building use

- lighting level for various types of use within an interior space
- ventilation standards
- energy efficiency standards
- safety and security issues

The building codes will regulate the design of the Building Refurbishment when the building professionals submit their plans to the local building authorities for approval. And only upon approval by the local building authorities would there be a set of certified building plans which are then used as part of the tender document to procure a contractor. In Singapore, all building works, except those that are minor and exempted under the schedule in its Building Control Act, will require building plan approval.

Barrier free code

In order to be an inclusive society, a lot of developed cities have adopted universal design. It advocates having building design for all sorts of people from the society instead of the general "average" person. This has a lot to do with the building codes since it regulates the minimum standard of building circulation space.

Creating a barrier free building means:-

- identifying the design features which could obstruct circulation or people movement
- be inclusive when designing such circulation and consider the whole range of people profile including the physically challenged
- evaluating the design including the smallest detail
- obtain feedback from building users and improve based on these feedback

The lack of barrier free accessibility poses a challenge for aging population, physically or visually handicapped and families with young children.

6.3   Planning Control

In Singapore and similarly in many parts of the world, building design is subject to planning control and approval. This is despite the different planning systems each country may have. Such approval controls the building development in terms of:-

- allowable use of the land/ building – residential, office, retail, industrial, hotel, mixed use, others etc.
- height of the building
- the architectural treatment e.g. the mass of the building, the orientation of the facing etc.
- conservation of part or whole of the building e.g. shophouses, old monuments, train stations, church buildings etc.
- owner's obligations in providing infrastructure e.g. underground access, link-bridge etc.

Planning control is a potential game changer which could either allow an investor to re-position or re-create a building or totally devastate any chance of renewing the building. Arising from such planning control, the building use, design and floor area of the intended Building Refurbishment are affected. Two of these factors – building use and floor area – in particular have a tremendous impact on economic feasibility. As you recall in Chapter 4, two of the most major asset enhancement strategies are

- increasing gross floor area which is achieved if the planning control allows more GFA
- increasing the rental rate which is achieved if the planning control allows a change of use

Sometimes the Building Refurbishment options are limited This further impacts the economic feasibility of the refurbishment.

In the event that there is insufficient excess GFA to make use of for instance, the building owner would have to consider paying development charge. Again such decision impact the economic feasibility as there is now additional development cost.

Planning control is a potential game changer which could either allow an investor to re-position or re-create a building or totally devastate any chance of renewing the building.

One possible way to improve the economic feasibility is to consider a change of use. Assuming the next building use is of a "higher" use in another words one that fetches higher rental income, it then fulfils asset enhancement strategy No. 2 "increasing rental rate". As you recall this is one of the two major ways to increase building value.

Change of use

Every land in Singapore has a land use designated by a statutory master plan. As such should the building owners wish to convert their building to another use e.g. from office to hotel or hotel/ office to residential, they would need to apply to the Singapore planning authorities and pay applicable development charge if allowed.

In recent years since the opening of the two Integrated Resorts in Singapore – Marina Bay Sands and Resort World Sentosa – tourist arrivals numbers has climbed steadily from 10 million in 2008 to the current 15 million in 2013. Hence it makes a lot of economic sense for building owners to convert their buildings to hotel. This is exactly what happened and an opportunistic window was available for the building owners to apply for a change of use before the Singapore planning authorities start to tighten such applications.

The above change of use differs from the change of use that an individual owner or tenant seek when they wish to change the use of say a shop from salon to maid agency or food outlet.

A change of use is also not referring to the building owner renewing or re-positioning a building within the same type of building use. For instance if the building owner who own an office building on a land designated as "Commercial" wishes to convert part of the office building for instance, to retail, there is no development charge. This is because both office and retail use falls within the definition of "Commercial" land use in Singapore. Such "change" is also considered part of the asset enhancement strategy No. 2 "increasing rental rate" but is strictly not a "change of use" in the regulatory sense.

Change of use is very common in building refurbishment especially when dealing with conservation buildings or drastic change in environment. For instance The Fullerton Hotel was previously a key government building and at one time is the Singapore General Post Office. Upon the sale of the building and land of the now The Fullerton Hotel, the government re-designated the land for hotel use. This is a case of a strategic direction by the government particularly in downtown area which warrant special attention in its downtown urban planning.

Another example is the current Capitol development in Singapore located right next to a downtown MRT station called "City Hall". This is part of a land sale by the Singapore government to rejuvenate the area and comprises four buildings on site. Three of the buildings are conserved buildings. See Figure 6.1 on Capitol Development.

As mentioned in the earlier section, Singapore experienced tremendous growth of tourist even after the opening of these two integrated resorts. Such phenomenon created a tremendous demand for hotel rooms. As such a lot of shophouses or office buildings were converted (change of use) to either hotel or hostel. An example is "The Sultan" hotel. See Figure 6.2 on The Sultan hotel and its explanatory notes.

Josh Ng

Figure 6.1 - Capitol Development in Singapore

2 Jun 2009 - Capitol Centre , Capitol Theatre, Capitol Building. Stamford Building which is not in this picture is sold together with the these three buildings and their land parcel in 2010 to be developed into a mixed development.

Capitol Centre building was demolished to make way for a high end residential and retail building.

Figure 6.2 - The Sultan hotel in Singapore

1- a total of 9 shophouses are amalgamated to form The Sultan hotel
2- the open courtyard and alley between the shophouses are used as circulation
3- the rooftop of the shophouses are used as roof garden and restaurants
4/5- interesting hotel rooms are created at the loft level with skylights

However one may note that additional cost is involved in the restoration of conserved buildings. This is due to several reasons:-

- Uncertain or little knowledge about the existing structural design and may require structural strengthening
- Special building materials may be required
- Government conservation guidelines may impose a higher construction cost to meet the restoration guidelines
- The structural grid and existing conserved building design may be inflexible and not fit for the purpose of the new use
- Conserved building refurbishment usually involves special construction technology for example façade retention, underpinning, micro-piling etc.

If carried out properly, conserved building refurbishment can create a win-win situation for everyone:-

- If the conserved building is a sold by the government for a private developer to redevelop into a new building, the government is relieved from the need to upkeep these buildings. In addition the government received a large sum of fund for the sale of the building (for a limited lease of say 99 years) and also created a stream of tax income through property tax.
- The new building owner would have created an unique product that could well differentiate itself from the competitors for example a 6 star hotel in a heritage building.
- The users of the new building would have a unique user experience
- The general public could still appreciate the beauty of the restored building and maintain a certain sense of the past.

In summary, a "change of use" could have various meanings as follows:-

Possible "levels" of "change of use"	Planning control regulatory requirements	Impact on Building Refurbishment creating higher building valve
Change of use for an interior space from e.g. a salon to a food outlet	Minimal or no planning control	Minimal change. Change only in terms of trade mix and have marginal impact on building value
Change of use for a building within the same zoning or master plan use e.g. from a outlet mall to a luxury mall	Minimal	Fulfils asset enhancement strategy No. 2 "increasing rental rate". Will increase the building value
Change of use for a building from one use to another .e.g from an office building to a hotel	Requires approval and/ or payment of development charge	Fulfils asset enhancement strategy No. 2 "increasing rental rate". Will increase the building value

Change of use for a conserved or heritage building by the government	Typically directed by the government and pre-approved for a change of use before being developed by private developer	Does not strictly fall within any asset enhancement strategies as the building valve is not enhanced by the owner but rather by the government. Any reasonable redevelopment of the conserved building would create value
Change of use for a conserved or heritage building by private building owners	Requires approval and/ or payment of development charge	Fulfils asset enhancement strategy No. 2 "increasing rental rate". Will increase the building value

6.4   Summary

All buildings are required to comply with regulatory requirements. Building Refurbishment projects are not exceptions. The major regulatory compliance are fire code, building code, barrier free code and planning control. Planning control is a potential game changer which could either allow an investor to re-position or re-create a building or totally devastate any chance of renewing the building. The concept of "change of use" itself needs to be understood carefully as there could be various interpretations.

CHAPTER 7

Project Management Issues In Building Refurbishment

Learning Objectives

*   To be able to assess the possible issues involved for Building Refurbishment from its project inception to completion

7.1 Building Refurbishment process

Figure 7.1 Building Refurbishment process

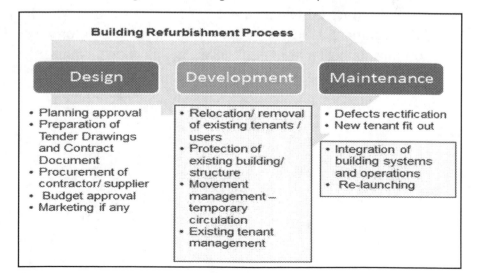

Building Refurbishment goes through a process that is not too different from the usual building cycle- Design, Development, Maintenance. The difference lies in the extent of the activities required for its design phase and the different emphasis during its development phase and to a certain extent its maintenance phase. Building Refurbishment development phase focuses on the following activities arising from the nature of the work:-

- relocation or removal of existing tenants or users
- protection of existing building or structure and sometimes even further enhance it
- movement management – creating temporary circulation to facilitate Building Refurbishment
- managing existing tenants

In the maintenance phase upon the completion of the Building Refurbishment project, the commercial building owners would have to consider:-

- integrating the building systems and operations of the old and new part of the building
- re-launching the building or the newly refurbished part of the building

The difference between new construction and Building Refurbishment activities based on the development process is summarised in Table 7.1 as follows:-

Table 7.1 – Difference between New Construction and Building Refurbishment

Development process	New Construction	Building Refurbishment (Commercial Buildings)
Market research and pre-planning	Based on the entire building	Could be either a repositioning of the building or focused on part of the building
Land acquisition	Required	Not required
Assembling the consultant team	Same requirements for both new construction and building refurbishment	
Planning / Building plan submission and approval	Required	Have the same requirements as new construction only if structural works is involved. Internal re-configuration does not require planning or building plans submission and approval unless there is a regulatory change of use
Marketing of properties	Usually for the whole building	May be focused on certain part of the building only

Procurement of contractors/ suppliers	Typically require structural, mechanical and electrical, architectural, piling works	May have specialist suppliers or contractors eg acoustic, façade, lighting etc in addition to those typically required for new construction
Construction	Typically on open land	As there could be existing occupants, special attention is made for managing the existing building
Temporary Occupation Permit / Certificate of Statutory Completion / Tenant Fit Out / Post Occupancy activities	Same requirements for both new construction and building refurbishment	

7.2   What are the unique characteristics of Building Refurbishment process?

What is uniquely Building Refurbishment is that it involves part or whole of an existing building and sometimes involves a **"live" building**.

What is uniquely Building Refurbishment is that it involves part or whole of an existing building and sometimes involves a "live" building. This concept of "live" building is mentioned in Chapter 6. It means that an existing building which is under refurbishment has existing tenants or users within the building during the refurbishment process. This is not ideal from the safety and project management's perspective. But it is inevitable if the building cannot be shut down, for example, an existing airport. In another situation, the commercial building owner may wish to maintain a certain level of rental revenue while the building is undergoing refurbishment. This is common for a mall refurbishment. This is because certain part of the mall has on-going leases and cannot be pre-maturely terminated. As such a mall refurbishment is typically done in phases to coincide with lease expiries if possible. It is precisely because of such situation of having to refurbish a "live" building that is where some of the issues arise.

The other characteristic is that Building Refurbishment involves part or whole of an existing building. The implications arising from such situation are many but not insurmountable. We will examine the issues involved in Building Refurbishment arising from these two characteristics.

As a recap, Building Refurbishment projects have two characteristics which are unique:-

- Issue 1 – sometimes dealing with "live" building
- Issue 2 – Building Refurbishment may involve either part or whole of the building

7.3   Issue 1 – Dealing with "live" building

In a "live" building there would be existing tenants, shoppers, users or deliveries etc. accessing and leaving the building while the Building Refurbishment is going on. As such, risk management is even more crucial in such Building Refurbishment projects. By managing the safety and environment, users would be ensured of any unnecessary loss of life or injuries. This is also to minimize inconvenience to ensure that building would be "business as usual" and hence minimize users compliant. This comes in the form of minimizing noise, dust and vibration during construction or carrying out the construction outside the operating hours. Such hours vary from building to building. For instance, the construction hours for shopping malls are likely to be after 10pm till 10am. It also depends on the neighbouring buildings – whether there are residential buildings or hotels nearby etc.

As such the refurbishment progress can sometimes be very slow as they are carried out in stages to existing building with existing users. Moreover as the Building Refurbishment progresses the building circulation and access are also affected and temporary circulation is often provided. Such temporary circulation will also be re-designed or shifted as and when the refurbishment project develops.

Parallel occupancy program

Especially in the context of a REIT's asset enhancement initiative, the asset manager would want a mall to run parallel with the Building Refurbishment project. Sometimes it is not possible to shut down a building as there are running tenancy agreements of varying expiry dates. As such an occupancy program runs parallel with the refurbishment construction program. This involves timing the expiry of the tenancy agreements of a certain section of the building. It could also be phasing the building refurbishment to systematically refurbish the building without affecting too much of the building operation and tenant's business. There must be sufficient notice for evacuation and relocation of facilities and building services. At times the tenants may be relocated to a temporary location before shifting back to its permanent location.

In summary carrying out Building Refurbishment in a "live" building requires a lot of work and planning. Time cannot be of an essence in such situation. Detailed project management is required to ensure that the existing building users can continue to use the building while Building Refurbishment is carried out. This involves:-

- mini phasing of work to suit the lease expiry or work sequence
- sufficient hoarding, protection of existing structure and environment
- noise insulation and protection against dust and vibration
- managing user and car movement in the form of temporary or permanent circulation or manual directing of traffic
- working and planning the work activities outside the building operating hours
- parallel occupancy program

7.4 Issue 2 - Building Refurbishment may involve either part or whole of the building

The nature of Building Refurbishment is very varied as explained in Chapter 2. Building Refurbishment could have "low", "medium" or "high" intervention to the building's façade or structure. The situation is tricky when the building to be refurbished is a heritage building. It is also tricky when we carry out Building Refurbishment to only one part of the building. The reason being that unlike new construction, building refurbishment projects starts with the analysis of an existing building. However often there is a lack of existing building information especially heritage buildings. As a result the structural strength of the existing building could not be easily determined. This poses a risk in the design of the Building Refurbishment scheme. Some other factors are:-

- difficult sites eg near to MRT, tight access
- poor quality of existing building
- existing structural capacity inadequate
- existing thermal and fire safety standards difficult to update
- existing dampness, insect, fungal and termite attack
- government restriction on conversation buildings

Some of the ways or sources to investigate further the existing building design are:-

- archives – as-built drawings, building documentations e.g. operating manual, statutory approval and certificates, suppliers and contractor list etc.
- detailed and on site survey or measurement and testing to check on building strength, site conditions, building conditions, tenant activities, site access
- engage professional surveyors to produce a detailed building survey report, asset listing etc.

The more thorough the initial investigation, the greater is the reliability of the planning and hence the project cost and execution and completion of the Building Refurbishment.

Structural Integrity

As Building Refurbishment is carried out in an existing building, the structural integrity of the existing building must be maintained at all times even during the construction period. Several structural considerations are required depending on the scope and location of building refurbishment. Some of the structural integrity considerations are discussed in Chapter 2 when we talked about building extensions.

Demolition

Partial demolition is expected in major building refurbishment. The three main areas of concerns are:-

- management of outgoing/ affected tenants or users
- structural integrity of existing structure
- noise and disturbance

Clearly any demolition work can only proceed after the existing tenants/ users have vacated the premise. This involves timely planning as the demolition planned should coincide with the expiry of tenant's lease if possible in order to avoid unnecessary loss of rental income. In addition all necessary pre-construction activities e.g. the planning approval, procurement of contractor should all be done prior to lease expiry in order to commence demolition on time. This is to minimize loss of project time.

Structural integrity of the existing structure in the building must be upheld at all times. A demolition of part of the building could shift the load transfer and result in structural cracks and even building collapse. As such approval should be sought from a professional structural engineer and also temporary structural support may be necessary.

Structural integrity of the existing structure in the building must be upheld at all times.

All demolition would generate tremendous noise, dust and vibration to the immediate tenants / users nearby. The local building or environment authorities would have stipulated certain maximum noise level for construction and demolition. This has to manage appropriately to minimize inconvenience and loss of goodwill.

7.5   Integration of the old and new

Perhaps what is also uniquely Building Refurbishment is how the new integrates with the old. How would the building be re-presented as an integrated whole? The integration of the old and new is to ensure that the building function as per the new design and Building Refurbishment scheme. It is inevitable given that Building Refurbishment would involve part or whole of an existing building.

Josh Ng

Some of the specific issues in the integration of old and new are:-

- building services connection and integration – the newly refurbished part of the building would of course requires building services – air conditioning, heating, plumbing, electrical, telecommunication etc. How could these services be connected to existing system to ensure continuity?
- levelling – at times the floor level of the old and new part of the building could not match though it would be ideal to do so. Hence other mitigation measures are required for example – ramps, steps or small escalators.
- use of finishes – unless there is a deliberate design for the newly refurbished part of the building to stand out from the rest of the building, the floor, wall and ceiling finishes adopted should be similar to the existing part of the building
- Character of the old and new- how does the newly refurbished part of the building complement the existing building?
- Use of frame and structures – typically structural steel frame system is used especially for building extensions as it provides the structural rigidity and yet is light weight as compared to reinforced concrete
- Structural integrity – as discussed in Section 7.4 and Chapter 2

How would the building be represented as an integrated whole? **The integration of the old and new** *is to ensure that the building function as per the new design and Building Refurbishment scheme*

7.6 Other issues in Building Refurbishment in the design phase

Some of the technical considerations during the design phase which are more challenging in a Building Refurbishment project as compared to new construction are:-

- challenges in regulatory compliance for an old building – fire safety code, accessibility code, green building, building control regulation, planning regulations etc. See Chapter 6
- design aspects –
  - how to position the new space
  - new internal layout
  - daylight penetration
  - aesthetics
  - form of construction – compatible with the original building ?
  - interface of the old and new
  - weather-tightness
  - impact on circulation

After the initial investigation and preliminary design, the building owner together with the consultant team would:-

- assess the conversion potential of the existing building in terms of marketability and functionality of new space, structural and technical possibility and economic feasibility
- determine the extent of demolition and new space
- produce preliminary refurbishment options as well as cost and timeline

Assuming a decision is made on the final refurbishment option, a process of clarification or submission with authorities begins. This involves:-

- clarification of initial design in more details
- preliminary planning and authorities submission
- obtaining authorities approval
- producing detailed drawings - architectural, structural, mechanical and electrical engineering, specialist drawings e.g. façade
- obtaining preliminary project cost and seeking budget approval
- obtain final authorities approval
- confirmation of final drawings and contract documents e.g. specifications

7.7   Building Refurbishment and project management team

A successful building refurbishment project relies heavily on the capable execution of a well-defined project objective that is aligned with the envisaged outcome. As the nature of the construction is very fragmented and is multi-disciplinary, proper allocation of responsibilities and coordination of all efforts would contribute to the project's success. A good understanding of the project management issues pertaining to Building Refurbishment and the risk management required further add to the project's success.

The main players in the project team are:-

- client / building owner
- support functions from the building owner
- consultant team
- contractor / suppliers

Other players who may have an impact:-

- government / authorities
- existing or new tenants/ users
- and even the public

For building owner, he makes important decisions on:-

- budget and payment
- design approval
- approval for variation to the design and scope

The owner's supporting functions will also have a large influence on the refurbishment. Their main supporting functions are:-

- Marketing department (for commercial properties refurbishment)
  - advise and influence the layout and floor area allocated for the new commercial space as well as the aesthetic feel
  - may have special request e.g. the installation of advertisement billboards or LED panels or incorporating atrium or event space
  - may have special request in terms of ceiling height, floor loading or building services for pre-committed tenant

- Maintenance / Operations department
  - advise on the impact on maintenance and operations and how best to incorporate the new space in order to have a better integration
  - advise on existing building conditions, traffic and building systems and brands adopted
  - will have a lot of involvement in terms of coordinating and directing the protection of existing structure, tenant management and traffic control

Consultant Team

Regardless of new construction or refurbishment, the consultant team would comprise of architect, structural engineer, mechanical and electrical engineer, project manager, quantity surveyor and specialist. The difference being:-

- architect – need to interpret the vision of the building owner for the new space and balanced it with authorities planning control which may sometimes not be aligned.
- structural engineer – as the refurbishment is to integrate with the existing building structure, careful planning and design is required to ensure structural integrity.
- M&E engineer – needs to consider the integration of the old and new M& E systems
- QS – needs to consider additional cost arising from tenant management measures, site access and higher contingency sum.

Contractor / Suppliers

The contractor selected should have a track record of refurbishment projects. This is because such contractor would better appreciate the nature of the refurbishment project and is then more cooperative.

Depending of the type of refurbishment project certain specialist suppliers may be sought. For example for a re-façade project, only certain specialist contractor with curtain wall or façade supply contact would be able to do the job. Another example is a restoration project which requires specialist tradesman.

Project management focus

The role of a project manager is even more critical in a building refurbishment project as compared to new construction. He handles multiple issues besides technical issues unlike new construction or infrastructure project. Every Building Refurbishment project is different and the project team which is usually led by the project manager should focus on certain aspects of project management that is catered to the site or project.

Project management is about managing three important project factors – time, cost and quality. In a commercial properties refurbishment, time management is critical as the earlier the refurbishment is completed the sooner rental income is collected. It can sometimes also be tied to certain terms and conditions attached with the securing of an anchor tenant e.g. the opening of the store. In this respect, the relocation or removal of existing tenants needs to be coordinated properly with the relevant operational department to ensure timely commencement of project. As such there needs to be very exhaustive preparation and planning even to the extent of hour to hour planning. Realistic contingency must be built in and fast management decision is required.

In other types of commercial Building Refurbishment the focus may be on meeting quality standard and less on keeping to the time and cost targets. This is the case when the building owner is refurbishing a heritage building.

Risk management

Another project management issue which is critical is risk management as part of the workplace safety and health compliance. Similar to other construction project, workplace safety and health is of utmost importance to prevent unnecessary loss of lives and damage to properties. A common practice is to adopt risk management. This is about:-

- identifying the risk
- measuring the risk – probability of happening & magnitude of loss/ gain

- overcoming the risk – prevention measures, workplace safety and health policy etc

It is not the intention of this book to elaborate on construction risk management. Rather this book highlights the risk management that is unique to Building Refurbishment.

Some of the possible commercial risks are:-

- continuing existence of the building / assets throughout the project duration – 'live' building
- unclear objectives of the refurbishment scheme
- cashflow of project
- strict timeline e.g. scheduled opening of a major store

Some of the possible project challenges are:-

- confined sites
- building may not be in good condition due to obsolescence or deterioration
- regulatory compliance for old buildings
- regulatory requirements for heritage or conserved building
- lack of building information
- unforeseen site conditions or project requirements
- interaction of old and new
- quality of workmanship
- weather protection during refurbishment
- access and circulation for users and also for the construction team and equipment movement

7.9   Building Refurbishment issues in the marketing phase

There isn't really a "marketing" phase per se as marketing should be done almost as soon as the refurbishment scheme is conceived. It can even be a trigger for Building Refurbishment as a major tenant may wish to take up space in a mall and the mall owner may refurbish the mall to accommodate the request. This is the case of Orchard Building and Hereen in Singapore Orchard Road. Both buildings were refurbished to accommodate a major anchor tenant – H&M flagship store for Orchard Building and Robinson store for Hereen.

Some of the major marketing events for commercial Building Refurbishment are:-

- marketing of the new space
- re-launching the property

Marketing of the new space

Just like any other new construction, the marketing of the new space created after the Building Refurbishment should carry out as soon as possible. This is primarily because if tenants are pre-committed to the new space, the rental income of the new space could be more established which makes the feasibility studies more reliable.

This is subject to:-

- the type of building being refurbished – e.g. a shopping mall would usually have pre-conceived retail concepts or retail mix. Marketing efforts can only be carried out once these concepts are established

- the type of tenancy arrangement
  - if the refurbished space is speculative in nature i.e. there is no pre-determined tenants in mind, then the marketing team would need to know the likely completion date in order to inform the prospective tenant
  - if an anchor tenant is already secured and the refurbishment is to cater to the anchor tenant, then the marketing effort has already been done.

The sequence of refurbishment process would be different

- all technical specifications are available eg floor area, building services capacity etc

- an assumption that existing tenant/ occupants would move out and all planning approval are obtained

Re-launching

Re-launching of a property after refurbishment depends on the original objective of the project. It could be a re-launching of the part of the building being refurbished or a re-positioning of the entire building. This is done with various forms of advertising and promotion or press release. In the case of institutional building it could a simple completion ceremony with press coverage.

7.10   Building Refurbishment issues in the post-occupancy phase

In the post occupancy phase of a Building Refurbishment, the maintenance team would probably need to work with the construction team to work on the following four aspects:-

- defects rectification
- revision of maintenance operations
- integration of the new and old maintenance system
- traffic flow and circulation

Defects rectification

Upon the completion of a Building Refurbishment project, there is usually a defects liability period ("DLP") of about 12 months for contractor to rectify any defects of the construction which does not meet the intended performance requirement. DLP is a useful period to evaluate how effective the various building systems and design in the refurbishment project is turning out as it does not cost the owner anything.

While the DLP would take care of the proper functioning of the technical aspects of the refurbishment, what it cannot rectify is the real estate aspects of the building – positioning, space efficiency, traffic flow etc. Once the refurbishment is completed it cannot be easily undone.

Revision of maintenance operations

There could be the following changes in the maintenance operations after the refurbishment completion:-

- increase area of maintenance
- additional new assets or equipment to maintain
- new tenants requirements – e.g. air conditioning hours for those shop units which operate 24 hours would differ from the typical mall hours
- change in human or car traffic – and therefore the need to re-design the deployment of security guards
- integration of new building systems e.g. M&E systems
- new focus area e.g. A&P (advertising and promotion)

The maintenance team may undergo the following changes:-

- revised operation procedures
- increase manpower requirements
- require additional expertise

The above are the areas where the building owner would need to assess before the completion of the refurbishment in order to avoid teething problems in the initial stages.

Integration of the new and old maintenance system

Areas which require system integration are:-

- M&E equipments
- M&E operations
- building services eg carparking, security, cleaning
- tenant management
- finance and accounting management
- authorities matter eg property income tax, licensing etc

Traffic flow and circulation

With the completion of the refurbishment, human and car traffic within and outside the building may change. Most of the traffic flow change should have been anticipated. However there could be unexpected changes which may affect the intended performance or function of the building/ new structure. At other times, it could be a situation of initial high traffic arising from the novelty of the newly launched building. Whatever is the situation, it make sense to have some contingency plans in terms of additional ad-hoc manpower e.g. security and cleaning services in the initial phase of building re-launch until it is stabilized.

7.11   Critical success factors for managing Building Refurbishment

In summary Building Refurbishment project is only as good as the team. Some of the critical success factors for building refurbishment are:-

- a well-researched and clear vision of the intended new space/ building
- quality of design
- capable contractor
- strong and user-centric risk and project management

It also entails being mindful of the differences and unique characteristics of Building Refurbishment as compared to new construction. The two unique characteristics are:-

- Building Refurbishment may sometimes involve "live" building
- Building Refurbishment may only involve part or whole of the building

USEFUL LESSONS

Building Refurbishment is a valuable tool to create value for commercial buildings. It takes a skillful investor to be aware of the overall environments to renew or reposition or re-create the commercial building. Inevitably value creation for commercial buildings comes in four ways:-

- By increasing the building GFA (legally)
- By improving its efficiency
- By increasing its average rental rate
- By reducing the building operating income

One of the most compelling factors to monitor is the commercial building's immediate competing commercial buildings. In particular the new commercial buildings built within 1km of the commercial building's vicinity. As shown in Singapore's Orchard Road and Marina Bay area examples, there seems to be repercussion impact on older commercial buildings over the next few years after a major new commercial building is completed. This is especially so in a highly concentrated commercial zone. However further research and studies are required to validate such observation or hypothesis.

The extents of which the commercial building owner creates value using Building Refurbishment, depends on the extent of the intervention to the building's façade and structure. A "high-high" intervention usually involves change of use to re-create or re-position the commercial building in order to reap the highest benefit.

Some of the critical success factors would be to have a competent project team who could interpret and implement the Building Refurbishment sensibly. This means being mindful that Building Refurbishment may sometimes involves a "live" building. It could also be for certain parts of the building. There will also be regulatory compliance issues as old buildings may have difficulties complying with newer codes.

By developing and implementing a refurbishment scheme that is feasible economically and is also practical and achieves the scheme's intended utility, a commercial building owner can increase their building's real estate value.

REFERENCES

Piyush Tiwari, Michael White (2010). *International Real Estate Economics*. Palgrave Macmillan.

Andrew Baum, Nick Nunnington, David Mackmin (2011, May 11). *The Income Approach To Property Valuation*. Estates Gazette 6th edition

Esther Teo (2012, Mar 1) *Turf City's new landlord plans to revive mall*. Retrieved from ST Property website on May 22, 2014

Suntec Real Estate Investment Trust (2011, Oct 31). *Remaking of Suntec City*. Retrieved from http://www.suntecreit.com/admin/ dir/2011103107102531Oct11%20Suntec%20REIT%20Announces%20 Remaking%20of%20Suntec%20City-%20Presentation%20Slides.pdf on Dec 22, 2014

Infopedia (2011). *Marina Bay Sands*. Retrieved from http://eresources. nlb.gov.sg/infopedia/articles/SIP_1607_20111101.html 1/ on Dec 16, 2014

James Douglas (2006). *Building Adaptation*. Butterworth-Heinemann 2nd Edition

David Kincaid (2002) *Adapting Buildings For Changing Uses*. Spon Press

Mike Riley and Alison Cotgrave (2011) *The Technology of Refurbishment and Maintenance*. Palgrave Macmillan

The Edge Singapore (2011, Mar 7) *CapitaMall Trust: Integration with Bugis Junction, asset enhancement to support Iluma buy*. The Edge Singapore

CapitaMall Trust (2008, May 22) *CMT signs agreement to acquire The Atrium@Orchard for S$839.8 million*. Press release by CapitaMall Trust

CapitaLand Inside (2013, Jan) *Plaza Singapura Now With A New Look and New Experiences*. Retrieved from http://inside.capitaland.com/spaces/leisure/1331plazasingapuranowwithanewlookandnewexperiences. on Dec 16, 2014

Marina Bay Sands (2014, Jul). *Marina Bay Sands Fun Facts*. Retrieved from http://www.marinabaysands.com/assets/Marina%20Bay%20Sands%20Fun%20Facts.pdf on Dec 22, 2014

Singapore Land Limited (2013, Apr 13) *Marina Square Reveals Plans For A New Gourmet Dining Zone And An Extensive New Retail Wing*. Press Release by Singapore Land Limited

Singapore Business Review (2013, Apr 13) *Bugis Junction to receive S$35m facelift for specialty store invasion*. Retrieved from http://sbr.com.sg/retail/news/bugisjunctionreceives35mfaceliftspecialtystoreinvasion on Dec 16, 2014.

The Straits Times (2011, Sep 2). *CityLink Mall to get $10m makeover*. The Straits Times

The Straits Times (2011, Jun 22). *CHIJMES A-CHANGING*. The Straits Times

The Business Times, Thursday (May 29, 2014). *One Raffles Place reopens today after major makeover*. The Business Times

Orchard Turn Developments Pte Ltd (2009, Mar 23) *ION ORCHARD TO OPEN FOR BUSINESS IN JULY.* Press release by Orchard Turn Developments Pte Ltd

Lend Lease (2011). *Lend Lease 313@somerset*
Retrieved from http://www.lendlease.com/asia/singapore/
projects/313somerset?
take=1&q=P2V2PTEsMCZyZWdpb249QXNpYS9TaW5nYXBvcmUv on
Dec 16, 2014

Wikipedia (2014, Dec 2). *Orchard Central.* Retrieved from http://
en.wikipedia.org/wiki/Orchard_Central on Dec 16, 2014.

Emilyn Yap (2008, Jul 23) *Palais Renaissance $16m facelift adds
sparkle.* Business Times Singapore.

CDL Hospitality Trust (2013, May 7). *CDL Hospitality Trust to unlock
value from Orchard Hotel Shopping Arcade with asset enhancement
plan.* Press release by CDL Hospitality Trusts.

Cheryl Ong (2014, Apr 17). *HPL land redevelopment 'can revive
Orchard belt's sleepy end'.* The Straits Times.

Wong Siew Ying (19 Nov 2014). *Can revamped Shaw Centre bring
buzz back to Scotts Road?* Channel News Asia

Jennani Durai (2013, Feb 22). *Revamp will link Shaw Centre to Shaw
House.* The Straits Times.

Elisabeth Gwee (2012, Mar 21). *Tangs to get makeover as it turns 80.*
The Straits Times.

Paragon (2008, Jan 7). *Facelift for Paragon to enhance retail
experience.* Retrieved from http://www.paragon.com.sg/chinese/press/
faceliftforparagontoenhanceretailexperience 3/ on Dec 16, 2014.

YTL Starhill Global Reit Management (2012, Sep 7) *Wisma Atria gets $31m revamp*. Quoted in The Straits Times Online.

AsiaOne (2012, Nov 29) H&M Ion Orchard opens to enthusiastic crowd. Retrieved from http://news.asiaone.com/News/Latest+News/Singapore/Story/A1Story20121129386497.html on Dec 16, 2014

OUE Limited (2013) *Mandarin Gallery*. Retrieved from http://www.oue.com.sg/ourentities/retailleasing on Dec 16, 2014

Alvin Yeo (2009, Nov 7) *Malls Get Bigger*. Retrieved from https://groups.yahoo.com/neo/groups/RealEdge/conversations/topics/12264 on Dec 22, 2014.

Kang Wan Chern of The Edge Singapore (2013, Apr 23) *Refreshing Robinsons*. The Edge Singapore.

Kalpana Rashiwala (2013, Dec 23) *TripleOne Somerset sold for $970m*. The Business Times

Perennial Real Estate Holdings Limited (2014) *Tripleone Somerset*. Retrieved from http://www.perennialrealestate.com.sg/properties/singapore/sgtripleonesomerset.html on Dec 16, 2014

Singapore Civil Defence Force (2013) *Fire Code 2013*

Singapore Building & Construction Authority, Building Control Act

Singapore Building & Construction Authority (2013). *Code on Accessibility In The Built Environment 2013*

Singapore Urban Redevelopment Authority. Development Control.

George Giebeler (2005) *Refurbishment Manual* .Birkhauser Verlag AG

Building & Construction Authority (2010) *Existing Building Retrofit*. Building & Construction Authority Singapore